EXECUTION EXCELLENCE

EXECUTION EXCELLENCE

MAKING STRATEGY WORK
USING THE BALANCED SCORECARD

SANJIV ANAND

WILEY

Cover design: Wiley

Published by John Wiley & Sons, Inc., Hoboken, New Jersey.
Published simultaneously in Canada.

For general information about our other products and services, please contact our Customer Care Department within the United States at (800) 762-2974, outside the United States at (317) 572-3993 or fax (317) 572-4002.

Wiley publishes in a variety of print and electronic formats and by print-on-demand. Some material included with standard print versions of this book may not be included in e-books or in print-on-demand. If this book refers to media such as a CD or DVD that is not included in the version you purchased, you may download this material at http://booksupport.wiley.com. For more information about Wiley products, visit www.wiley.com.

Library of Congress Cataloging-in-Publication Data:

Names: Anand, Sanjiv, author.
Title: Execution excellence : making strategy work using the balanced scorecard / Sanjiv Anand.
Description: Hoboken, New Jersey : John Wiley & Sons, Inc., [2016] | Includes index.
Identifiers: LCCN 2015048159| ISBN 9781119196464 (hardback) | ISBN 9781119196488 (ebk); ISBN 9781119196471 (ebk)
Subjects: LCSH: Balanced scorecard (Management) | Strategic planning. | BISAC: BUSINESS & ECONOMICS / Strategic Planning.
Classification: LCC HD58.93 .A53 2016 | DDC 658.4/012–dc23 LC record available at http://lccn.loc.gov/2015048159

10 9 8 7 6 5 4 3 2 1

This book is dedicated to my wife, Monica, and to my boys, Sahil and Jai, for tolerating my 30 years of travel in trying to make strategy work for clients.

To my dad, who taught me consulting and how to be a good human being. And to my mom, who helped my dad and me follow our dreams.

Contents

Preface

This is my second book. My father always encouraged me to write. He felt that it was a great way for people to share their experiences with others. As a management consultant, he had a number of stories that he loved to tell which encouraged me to follow the same career path. In an average year, a consultant goes through 10 client experiences, managing over 10 relationships with each client. That's 100 relationships a year, with another 100 added every year you're in the business. As a result, management consultants enjoy many more professional relationships than people in other jobs—more than some people cultivate over an entire lifetime. This wonderful opportunity also comes without your having to go to the same office every day. Almost every day, I'm in a different city, plane, taxi, office—even in a different time zone. It sounds tiring, but I don't regret a single day of what I have done in the past 30 years of my life, no matter how hard it has been.

And this book is that story. I have seen companies of all shapes and sizes in every part the world attempt to commit to being strategy-focused and performance-oriented organizations. From a major consumer electronics retailer in the United States and a duty-free operator in the United Kingdom, to a Georgian bank in Tbilisi and a family-owned business in Abu Dhabi, to a telecom company in India and a stock exchange in Singapore. Some succeed, some do moderately well, and some die.

This book is not about the theory of strategy and its execution; I don't have a PhD, and it's too late to get one. It is about strategy and its execution in the real world—and believe me, after all I have seen, it is clear that the real world is different than what books make it out to be. In some markets, the strategy can be complex. In other markets, the strategy is simple because the market is simple. Irrespective of the complexity of the market or the strategy, what matters is the execution. It's about getting the strategy executed, within the timelines you have, with the resources you can bring to the table to achieve the results you desire. That's execution excellence.

In my first 10 years executing strategy as a consultant, I did not use the Balanced Scorecard (BSC). Discovering the BSC overhauled my approach and in the years since, I have found time and again that there is no better framework to help you execute strategy successfully. That is what this book is about.

The material is presented in two distinct parts. The first explains how to design the BSC to execute your strategy, and the second covers how to ensure its successful implementation. To reach execution excellence, success in both areas is critical.

You will find many books on the subject of BSC or strategy execution. This one takes a practical approach, using real-world lessons to learn about what actually happens.

Enjoy the ride!

Acknowledgments

It would be impossible to write a book about execution excellence without thanking the clients I've had over my 30-year career. At last count, there were over 200 of them, across 30 different industries, in 25 countries, and of many nationalities. From young entrepreneurs to seasoned industrialists, from government executives to college deans, I thank you all. Thank you not only for the opportunity to work with you, but also for your trust and openness as you shared your thoughts with me. You have taught me so much about execution and business. Yes, I admit it. Consultants learn from their clients, and also pass that knowledge forward. Life and learning is always about interaction. As is this book.

None of this would ever have been possible without my colleagues. Consulting and execution of strategy is all about teamwork. Since my early days in Chicago, where I learned the art of consulting, to New York, Mumbai, Dubai, and infinite other locations, my colleagues have been next to me and our clients, making strategy work. Special thanks go to V. Ramkumar, Chetan Parekh, and Amit Jain, who have been with me through this process for over 10 years. My gratitude also goes to all my bosses who, since 1985, have also been my well-wishers. And lastly to one of my young consultants, Aditi Kothari, for having helped me through the process of completing this book.

And I do believe in God, so thank you, God, for the opportunities you have provided and the happiness that has come with them.

The Real World of Strategy

1

The Global Business Environment in Today's Flat World

News Flows Faster than Water!

The problem with writing about global business is that every-thing changes overnight. Today's topics are not even tomor-row's history or news. The Internet, information technology (IT), and the rapid globalization of businesses over the past 30 years have made this possible. So you have to excuse me if I make some comments today that may seem utterly meaningless a few years from now. However, the good news is that in spite of this, the topic of execution excellence will remain evergreen. It will continue to exist as long as human beings exist, and corporations exist with the intent to succeed. So, from that standpoint, your investment in this book is safe.

Now back to global business environment. I started my career as a young consultant back in Chicago in 1985. It wasn't easy. I remember one of my first clients, an industrial-crane manufacturer on the outskirts of Chicago, telling me that he wasn't going to take advice from a 26-year-old Indian kid with a funny accent. He even looked like Ronald Reagan, which made it more strange. What he didn't know was that my boss, sitting next to me, was actually of Iranian origin. Together, we fixed the company in four months, and in spite of the client's challenging demeanor, he publicly appreciated the work we had done. An Indian and an Iranian in the 1980s fixing a traditional midwestern manufacturing company. My first experience in a flat world!

It may seem a unique event, but our friend was clearly not paying attention to the world around him. In the late 1970s, the gutting of U.S. manufacturing started, and original equipment manufacturers (OEMs) seeking lower costs started moving plants to China. I remember those days clearly. On my way from one midwestern city to another, I drove through small-town America, and it was clear how plant closures were destroying local economies. Main Street shops were shuttered and pawn shops replaced them. I know this space well, because my colleagues and I facilitated this process. We helped a large number of Fortune 500 companies across industries set up operations across the world, mostly in China and India. I know that many people say that the globalization of business began centuries ago with ancient trading routes and has existed ever since. The shift also comes from modern Western companies globalizing over the years. But let's be honest, when we talk about globalization today, it's really a BRICS story, and particularly the China and India story

What started as an OEM movement soon overflowed to suppliers. If a large U.S. corporation set up a plant in China or India, you could hardly expect the suppliers to all be based in the Midwest. Soon the suppliers were being asked to set up operations in China, near the OEM plants. Many of the owners of these small and medium enterprises (SMEs), who had not even made frequent trips to New York, were now being asked to go set up shop in China. Some brave ones tried, and of those some succeeded but many did not. They hoped that their other customers would not do the same; however over a period of time, most did. A considerable proportion of the SME businesses died out and was soon replaced by local Chinese suppliers, who probably stole their technology. The large-scale manufacturing movement to international markets helped the large corporations survive, but killed many small and medium-sized businesses who didn't have the resources to compete.

Of course, low-cost manufacturing grew in emerging markets and created exports to high-demand markets. India built an entire IT industry that allowed for on-shoring and off-shoring of technology and business processes. Through all this outflow and inflow, the world became flat. Maybe this is what the original discoverers of the continents meant; Facebook and Google made it a permanent reality.

So Where Do We Go from Here?

All businesses today, whether local, global, or *glocal*, operate in a flat world. A small pharmaceutical manufacturer in India competes with local SME's, large national players, small and large regional players, and medium and large global players. Most of these competitors operate like Tomahawk missiles fired from a ship off shore. The small local players don't see them till they hit and by then it's too late. The same is true for many businesses. I'm not saying that these small business can't compete. In fact, often it's the large international players who underestimate the smaller competitors. All I'm saying is that the world is flat and that's how it's going to remain. So if one is writing a book about strategy and execution, it is obvious that this strategy will have to succeed in an environment of a flat world.

What Does That Mean?

1. From a financial perspective, it means that your financial endgame needs larger aspirations.
2. It means your revenue drivers will have to include organic and inorganic cross-border growth.

3. It means your financial risk will involve cross-border currency risks as well as benefits.

4. It means your cost and efficiency will need to be globally competitive, often having suppliers and employees off shore in locations you could not imagine.

5. Your customers will be global.

6. Your brand will have to translate into many languages and something globally meaningful.

7. Your relationship management skills will need to be much better than the U.S. airlines that we tolerate today.

8. Your products will need to be competitive across multiple customer segments.

9. Your innovation processes will need to design products and services for multiple markets.

10. Your sales engine cost structure will need to profitably sell high-value products in mature markets and low-value products in emerging markets.

11. Your organization will look like the UN, but will need to be performance driven.

12. Your IT will be the glue that holds your organization together and helps it deliver value.

If you are ready for all of the above, you are ready to execute strategy successfully in a flat world. Let's go do it!

2

The Evolving Role of Strategy

Is Strategy Dead?

I'm not a strategy guru. Neither am I a professor with a PhD. All I am is a simple practitioner of strategy, who has spent 30 years helping clients execute strategy globally in places you wouldn't want to go. For the consultants who complain about travelling to Chicago in the winter, how about trying to execute strategy in remote areas of India, China, or Pakistan, or better yet in Tbilisi, Georgia, with Russian tank turrets only a few miles away. For 30 years I have crisscrossed the globe helping clients execute strategy, and I have a big secret to share with you today. Actually, it's the elephant in the room: It's all about execution and making strategy work! It's not about the formulation.

So, is strategy dead? Not really. Remember, I said it's about making strategy work. To execute a strategy, one obviously needs a strategy in the first place. However the one thing I will say is that strategy is overrated. What's the point of having a strategy that can't be executed? You may know the old adage, "Don't fight a battle that you can't win." I like to apply it to my work by saying,

"Don't call something a strategy if you can't execute it." A non-executable strategy is meant for your bookshelf; maybe with all the other theoretical consultant reports you may have collected over the years.

Blue-Sky Strategy

There are plenty of words you can use to make basic things sound very interesting. Take for example words like *blue sky* or *moon shot*. They all sound really nice. To put it simply, it means something out-of-the-box, innovative—something aspirational that you want but don't know how to reach, and so on. Nothing runs with that and, I am sorry, you can't run a corporation on the basis of such a strategy. It can be one component of an overall strategy, but not the whole enchilada.

Have you ever seen a blue-sky strategy report (sometimes called a 30,000-feet report), or some of the reports of leading consulting firms. They all sound very logical, fancy, nicely charted, but can you execute the strategy? No way. There isn't enough detail to tell you how to move ahead. I don't mind it. That's what keeps firms like mine, and many others, alive. Clients hand us a report and say, "Here's what the board mandated and the consultants came up with. But we don't know how to execute it. Please help us." This means they still need a strategy that has the level of detail that needs to be executed, or an *operational strategy*.

Back-to-Basics Strategy

If you look at the origin of consulting firms, about a hundred years ago, they started with operational strategy. Many of them worked with clients to help them improve processes, manage costs, and drive enterprise performance. Over the years, starting in the

1960s, as management education evolved and the business schools starting turning out MBAs, and as companies began hiring them, management thinking started to evolve. All of a sudden, there was a burst of new management ideas, and the concept of strategy and strategic planning came into play. The fact that faculty of some of the leading business schools on the planet saw this as a revenue-generating opportunity for themselves, in terms of books and consulting contracts, accelerated the process. As the son of a professor and consultant—and a consultant myself—I don't think there's anything wrong with that. I'm just laying out in simple terms what I think about the evolution of the concept of strategy and the strategy planning process.

This definitely drove the evolution of new industry sectors (e.g. business services, information technology), but most importantly, it accelerated globalization overall. As discussed earlier, the era of the 1980s and 90s was the big bang era of globalization with China.

Unfortunately, since then life has become somewhat boring on the strategy formulation front. It's somewhat like the current trend of back-to-basics concepts in banking. Now that the banks have had all the fun they wanted, including huge bonuses and a near blow-up of the world's financial system, it's time to get back to the basics of retail and corporate banking: deposits and lending. Strategy has given us a lot of good things, but it's also given us a lot of bad habits, including the wave of mergers and acquisitions (M&A). A CEO may think M&As are the best thing since sliced bread, and turn around and sell everything off to concentrate on the core business—and life goes on. This has repeatedly been done in the past and many times destroyed enterprise value and hundreds of jobs.

I think we are now back to the basics in terms of strategy. CEOs and clients are looking ahead for an operational strategy that works. It will have many motherhood components, but there is nothing wrong with that. If you can't get the motherhood components right on a consistent basis, first focus on that. Once you get that right consistently, you may not even need the blue sky strategy. Some examples of motherhood components are:

- Achieving consistent financial performance
- Creating a culture for performance
- Creating a culture for sales excellence
- Consistently meeting or exceeding customer needs
- Consistently delivering processes
- Optimizing the organizational structure and headcount
- Creating a mobile organization

How many times have I seen clients want to achieve the above? Countless times over several decades. The goals are always the same. How come with all the advances in strategy and innovation, the goals stay the same? I think it's because the emphasis on sound operational strategy and execution has been lost along the way. It's time to get back to the basics, starting with the question: What does an operational strategy mean?

3

Strategy Formulation

Building a Strategy that Works

I'm not a strategy professor, but I can definitely tell you, from my perspective and experience, what strategy formulation is about and how to build a strategy that works. I'll keep it simple.

Strategy is all about understanding the three components, which are explained here and shown in Figure 3.1:

1. **External Assessment:** What's the relevant market and what does it offer in terms of opportunity? What are the market, competitive, regulatory, and other constraints or gaps?
2. **Internal Assessment:** What are our strengths, weaknesses, and resources?
3. **Way-Forward Strategy Formulation:** What do we need to do internally to successfully execute the external market opportunity?

It's as simple as that.

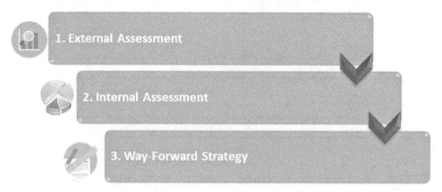

FIGURE 3.1   Strategy Components

External Assessment

There is no rocket science here, so I am not going to spend much time on this. In old-fashioned terms, an external assessment is *good old market research, market intelligence, competitive intelligence, market strategy*—they all mean pretty much the same thing. A strong external assessment involves reading everything there is about the market, so you have clear answers to questions listed above. Additionally to complete your understanding of the market, plan on meeting with a relevant number of customers, regulators, industry experts and competitors. This is particularly important as, everything outlined in today's Google world may not be entirely accurate.

I have conducted thorough research like this many times over the years, and I have realized that even mapping larger markets in the world, such as China, should not take more than 12 weeks to complete. Use external advisors as a force multiplier, if you want. Trust them but verify what they tell you.

Internal Assessment

This should be easier than the external assessment, because the information you need should ideally be at your fingertips, but over the years, I have found that it's surprisingly difficult to gather reliable internal information. In some cases, it's harder to get information from internal sources than from the market and even the competition.

A solid internal assessment requires pulling financial, customer, channel, product, process, organizational, and information technology (IT) data from within the organization. You would think with all the billions of dollars of investments in IT systems and databases, this information would all be readily available, but that's not true. It takes about eight weeks to pull together strategic data and verify its accuracy.

One important thing to remember is that the definition of a *client* could mean different things to different departments within the same organization. As you sort the data, it's important to understand the context as it applies to each source. Another challenge is the simple law of the corporate jungle that *information is power*. Even if certain information exists, you may be blocked from accessing it.

Once you get past these difficulties, it's time to augment the internal assessment data by having conversations with the management team. While everything that is written down may not be true, everything you need to know may not be written down. Here, too, the conversations are not easy, and office politics can be a stumbling block. People won't speak up unless they feel that the person they are talking to is knowledgeable, credible, and trustworthy. An outside consultant can help you establish rapport by moderating the conversation.

Get past all of the above barriers and in about 8 to 12 weeks you should have a strong internal and external understanding of what's going on. Then, it's time to document a way-forward strategy.

Strategy Formulation with the BSC

While the Balanced Scorecard (BSC) was designed as an execution tool, it really can help formulate the strategy also. Once you have completed a thorough internal and external assessment, try to summarize your objectives using the four BSC perspectives:

1. Define your financial strategy in terms of the overriding financial objective driven by a revenue strategy, a profit strategy, a risk strategy, and a cost strategy.
2. Define your customer and product strategy to meet your financial expectations in terms of your products/service strategy, your relationship strategy, and your brand strategy.
3. Define your process strategy in terms of innovation strategy, market strategy, sales and channel strategy, and delivery strategy.
4. Lastly define the learning and growth strategy, led by human resources (HR) and IT, that will help deliver your processes, ultimately delivering your customer and financial expectations.

At the end of this process, you should have 20–25 objectives that are integral to your strategy. These can be laid out in a Strategy Map as shown in Figure 3.2, which is an example Strategy Map for a real estate company looking to define its overall objectives and set course for growth.

So what you end up is with a really neat and simple strategy document of about 150 pages. The information usually breaks down as follows:

- About 30–40 pages of strategic review of the market, based on your external assessment.
- About 40–50 pages of a strategic internal review, based on your internal assessment.
- About 30 pages detailing the resulting strategy and objectives.
- About 10 pages covering next steps—how you will pursue that strategy.
- About 2–3 pages for the Strategy Map and Balanced Scorecard.

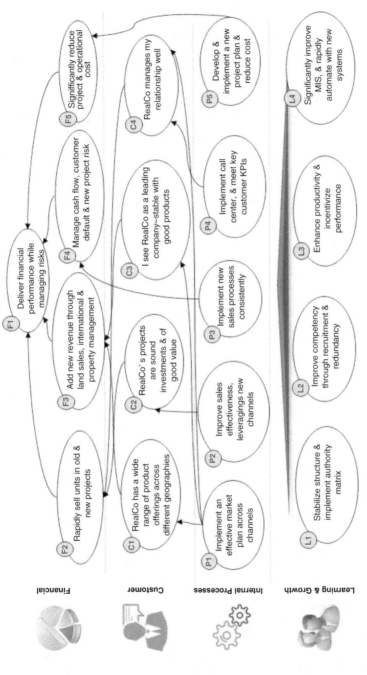

FIGURE 3.2 Real Estate Strategy Map Created Using BSC

Financial

- **F1** Deliver financial performance while managing risks
- **F2** Rapidly sell units in old & new projects
- **F3** Add new revenue through land sales, international & property management
- **F4** Manage cash flow, customer default & new project risk
- **F5** Significantly reduce project & operational cost

Customer

- **C1** RealCo has a wide range of product offerings across different geographies
- **C2** RealCo's projects are sound investments & of good value
- **C3** I see RealCo as a leading company–stable with good products
- **C4** RealCo manages my relationship well

Internal Processes

- **P1** Implement an effective market plan across channels
- **P2** Improve sales effectiveness, leveragings new channels
- **P3** Implement new sales processes consistently
- **P4** Implement call center, & meet key customer KPIs
- **P5** Develop & implement a new project plan & reduce cost

Learning & Growth

- **L1** Stabilize structure & implement authority matrix
- **L2** Improve competency through recruitment & redundancy
- **L3** Enhance productivity & incentivize performance
- **L4** Significantly improve MIS, & rapidly automate with new systems

15

The result is a strategy that works because your 20–25 objectives are focused, covering the four key BSC areas. The BSC and Strategy Map make it easy to operationalize these objectives and understand how the many strategic components relate to one another. Since you have used the BSC framework to summarize your strategy, you now have a *plug-and-play* opportunity. Your strategy document typically ends with a Strategy Map and a BSC and your execution document begins with the same. Now you are ready to execute your strategy.

4

Strategy Execution

It's All About the Implementation

We've talked extensively about greater need for an operational strategy, and the ability to execute it using the Balanced Scorecard (BSC) framework. Since the following chapters focus on the design and execution of a BSC, I want to make a few *strategic* comments here about what to expect during the process.

Here's my list of top 10 things an organization needs to get the execution right:

1. The top 20–25 strategic objectives should be clear.
2. They should be balanced, covering financial and non-financial aspects of the business.
3. The targets should be a balance between aggressive and realistic. Only a few should be aspirational. Remember you are running a marathon, not sprint. Companies are meant to live 100+ years.

4. The board, CEO, and management team should be aligned and believe the strategy can be executed. Remember don't fight a battle you can't win.

5. Most of the competencies of the existing employees can help deliver the strategy combined with some strategic hires to fill the gaps.

6. Your organization will get stretched in terms of its competencies, but your people know how to get there.

7. The execution should show some immediate results within the first year, with most of the results coming in by the third year. If you can't execute the strategy within three years for your core business, your long-term goals are dead.

8. You have a world-class project management office (PMO) to help manage the execution of strategy while the management team does the executing. The management team can't do both.

9. You have a great communication strategy—both internal and external—that follows the basic principles of good communication. Decide clearly what to communicate, when to communicate and how to communicate.

10. The organization is motivated enough that it wants to succeed, win, and, most importantly, *punch above its weight.*

5

The Business Planning Process

Don't Let the Process Overrun You

N owadays at some banks, the compliance team is larger than the relationship management team, and the paperwork often overwhelms the people. The same is often true with business planning and its process. It becomes an endless task, with infinite meetings and a parade of external facilitators. Rather than listening to their gut and employees, many management teams spend an excessive amount of time listening to consultants.

The process becomes so cumbersome that the budgets and the strategic planning process often don't match, and the process extends into the year that it is supposed to start delivering value.

When done correctly, the whole business planning process should not last more than a quarter. Figure 5.1 outlines the five simple steps of the business planning process.

I have a few simple recommendations on how to approach the business planning process, based on the Business Scorecard

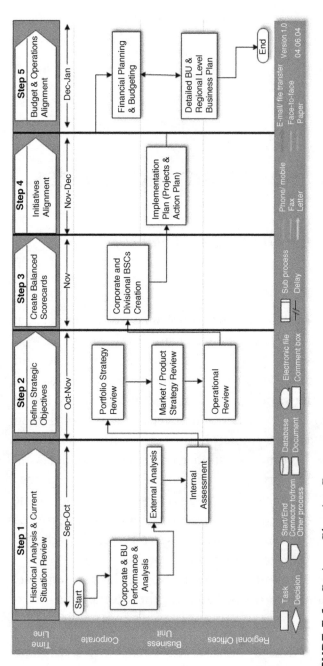

FIGURE 5.1 Business Planning Process

20

(BSC) framework. If you can make this work, you should be in good shape.

- Formulate your strategy, and set your top 20–25 financial and non-financial targets.
- Clearly define your list of the top 20 of projects/initiatives to help deliver your strategy. Compute the fiscal, people, and technology investments required to deliver them on time.
- Translate the above into a detailed budget document aligning both your strategy and financial plans at the enterprise level.
- Cascade your strategic planning and budgeting processes to the division or departmental level.
- Iterate between enterprise and department/divisional level budgets and strategy till both are aligned.
- Create individual performance measures that align to enterprise performance.

Ownership

Needless to say the *strategic planning unit*, along with any external advisors, owns the strategic planning process, but the ultimate ownership belongs to the CEO and the management team. This seems obvious, but you'd be amazed how many times I find the strategic planning head being put in a difficult spot when it comes to ownership and accountability. Hence, even if the strategic planning unit has done a great job of doing the analysis, pulling the deck together, and providing some strategic insights, the ultimate responsibility related to performance, or lack of it, is with the management team. Managers who understand this will not ask the strategic planning head questions about performance; but instead question themselves or those around the table.

Introducing the Balanced Scorecard

## 6

Introducing the Balanced Scorecard

Circa 1992 and Still Going Strong

History

Hundreds of professors, consultants, and thought leaders every year, come up with what they think is the next big management concept or idea. It has sort of slowed down in recent years, but the ideas still flow. As can be expected, ideas tend to come from the more renowned business schools and firms.

Around 1992, one such concept emerged from the research of Robert Kaplan, a Harvard Business School professor, and his associate David Norton, a business theorist and consultant. What they found was not surprising. Most firms are unable to execute strategy for a number of reasons, including lack of a clear vision, misaligned competencies, too much focus on financial perform-ance, and other pitfalls. Rather than focusing on building the next best mousetrap in terms of strategy formulation, Kaplan and Norton focused on building a framework for strategy execution. That makes sense. *What's the point of having a strategy if you can't make it work?* The result is what is now known as the Balanced Scorecard (BSC).

In 2015, I can still write a book about a concept introduced in 1992. That shows how valuable Kaplan and Norton's work is. Many management ideas have come and gone in the past, many have a sell-by date because they rely too heavily on trends that disappear. If you talk to companies around the world about what framework they currently use to execute strategy, many will tell you they rely on the BSC. Even the well-known global consulting firms, in spite of being intellectual powerhouses, more often than not will use the BSC, as opposed to developing their own tools and theories, to help clients execute strategy. Successfully executing strategy is critical to the success of most firms; this chapter elaborates how best to use the BSC to make this happen.

Basic BSC Framework

Plenty of books have been written on the subject, so I am going to dispense with the theory, and do a quick and dirty introduction to the BSC. Then, we can move on to the more interesting stuff.

The BSC has two key pages. The first is a *Strategy Map*. A Strategy Map identifies the top 20–25 strategic objectives that a firm is seeking to execute in the four key areas of finance, customer, process, and learning and growth. You've seen a sample strategy map in Chapter 3. Figure 6.1 provides another example, this time in the banking industry.

Many times, a first look makes this map seem a lot more complex than it really is. Some clients find it too unwieldy and detailed, but with some time and coaching they will understand how this document makes their lives easier. As we move ahead in this book, you will draw these better than I can for your firm.

The second key page is the BSC itself, which has a tabular format (Figure 6.2). There's no rocket science here. Each

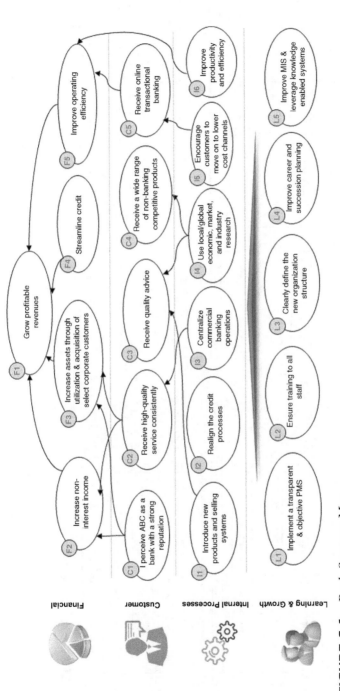

FIGURE 6.1 Bank Strategy Map

Financial

- F1 Grow profitable revenues
- F2 Increase non-interest income
- F3 Increase assets through utilization & acquisition of select corporate customers
- F4 Streamline credit
- F5 Improve operating efficiency

Customer

- C1 I perceive ABC as a bank with a strong reputation
- C2 Receive high-quality service consistently
- C3 Receive quality advice
- C4 Receive a wide range of non-banking competitive products
- C5 Receive online transactional banking

Internal Processes

- I1 Introduce new products and selling systems
- I2 Realign the credit processes
- I3 Centralize commercial banking operations
- I4 Use local/global economic, market, and industry research
- I5 Encourage customers to move on to lower cost channels
- I6 Improve productivity and efficiency

Learning & Growth

- L1 Implement a transparent & objective PMS
- L2 Ensure training to all staff
- L3 Clearly define the new organization structure
- L4 Improve career and succession planning
- L5 Improve MIS & leverage knowledge enabled systems

27

Obj. #	Objective		Measure	Unit	Freq.	Objective Owner	MTD Actual	MTD Target	YTD Actual	YTD Target
FINANCIAL										
F1	Grow profitable revenues	1	Net profit as % of total commercial income	%	M	CEO				
		2	Commercial income growth	%	M	CEO				
F2	Increase non-interest income	1	Non-interest income as % of total income	%	M	CEO				
F3	Increase assets through utilization & acquisition of select corporate customers	1	Growth in funded assets book	%	M	CEO				
		2	New select corporate customers acquired	No.	Q	Head – Corporate Banking				
F4	Streamline credit	1	Average turnaround time of approval	Days	Q	CRO				
F5	Improve operating efficiency	1	Oper. cost as % of total commercial income	%	M	COO				
CUSTOMER										
C1	perceive ABC as a bank with strong reputation	1	Customer Index	Index	Y	Head – Retail & Corporate Banking				
C2	Receive high-quality service consistently	1	Customer Satisfaction Index	Index	Y	Head – Retail & Corporate Banking				
C3	Receive quality advise	1	Funded Utilization	%	Q	CRO				
		2	Average RM calls per customer	No.	Q	Head – Branches				
C4	Receive a wide range of non-banking competitive products	1	Customer Index	Index	Y	Head – Retail & Corporate Banking				
C5	Receive online transactional banking	1	New online services launched	No.	HY	Head – Channels				
		2	Customer Satisfaction Index	Index	Y	Head – Retail & Corporate Banking				
INTERNAL PROCESS										
I1	Introduce new products, and selling systems	1	% revenue from new products	%	Y	Head – Retail & Corporate Banking				
		2	Revenue from sales of retail products	USD	Q	Head – Retail Banking				
I2	Realign the credit processes	1	KMS for streamlining credit	No.	M	CRO				
I3	Centralize commercial banking operations	1	KMS for organization restructuring	No.	M	CEO				
I4	Use social/global economic, market, and industry research	1	KMS for research cell setup	No.	M	CRO				
		2	Research reports made available	No.	Q	CRO				
I5	Encourage customers to move on to lower cost channels	1	% of total transactions done through electronic channels	%	M	Head – Channels				
		2	Accounts exited/transferred to Retail as % of total accounts	No.	Q	Head – Channels				
I6	Improve productivity and efficiency	2	Education/Communication exercises to customer	%	Q	CEO				
LEARNING & GROWTH										
L1	Implement a transparent & objective PMS	1	KMS for performance management system	No.	M	HR HEAD				
L2	Ensuring training to all staff	1	Training man days per FTE	No.	Y	HR HEAD				
L3	Clearly define the new organization structure	1	KMS for organization restructuring	No.	M	CEO				
L4	Improve career and succession planning	1	Employee satisfaction survey	Index	Y	HR HEAD				
		2	Revenue per employee	USD	Y	CEO				
		3	Employee Turnover	%	M	HR HEAD				
L5	Improve MIS & leverage knowledge enabled system	1	User Requests	No.	M	Head – IT				
		2	New MIS Reports Available	No.	Q	Head – IT				

FIGURE 6.2 Bank BSC

objective has associated measures that allow you to track your progress. It also designates an owner for each objective. This makes it clear who is responsible and if the plan is being executed as planned.

The list of objectives from the strategy map is in the leftmost column. The associated measures used to track progress are in the following column followed by units of measure, frequency, actuals, targets, and a link to identify the initiatives being deployed to ensure delivery of strategy. The responsible individual is also named for each objective.

If you'd like to round out your BSC, you can add a few pages, such a table tracking the progress of key initiatives and a discussion about next steps. The beauty of it is that if you keep it simple, it can be amazingly effective in helping you track your performance on delivering strategy on a focused basis. The key is to keep your focus on executing the strategy and not let running the BSC become the endgame.

Design

Designing the strategy map and BSC can seem complex, but if you have a good strategic mind and a team of the key executives in the room who need to own the delivery of strategy, it can be done in a reasonable amount of time. I've designed them for Fortune 500 companies and find that 8–12 weeks is sufficient. In the heady early days of the BSC, the programs could run longer than four months. I honestly believe that the problem came from consultants who were eager to make more money than any need for the program to run that long. That being said, it's better to have an expert help with the design so you get it right the first time without any internal political pressures. In short, bring in a consultant, but be clear about your needs and timeline.

Implementation

Once the design is done, it should take no more than 45–60 days to get it up and running. The typical approach is a monthly management meeting with all key executives in the room, using the BSC to review monthly performance, with the BSC coordinator facilitating the meeting. The meeting should last for no more than a couple of hours, and it really needs to be a focused discussion on performance, what's blocking it, and how can that be fixed.

Cascades

Cascading is building BSCs for the business units or key functions. The design and implementation process is more or less the same, and the designs could be light or regular depending upon the situation. These BSCs could seem more operational in terms of objectives because as you go deeper into an organization, the objectives can become less strategic and more operational. The cascades are typical owned and run by the business units and functions they were built for.

Individual BSC

The primary objective of the BSC was to focus on enterprise rather than individual performance. It was really designed for the CEO or business head, and the strategic planning unit. However, over time, since driving individual performance was observed to drive enterprise performance, the human resources (HR) folks picked up on the framework. Today, my assessment is that in at least 50 percent of the cases worldwide, the BSC is being used primarily to focus on individual performance management. That being said, HR has gotten a bit carried away, which is why you

Sr. No	Perspective	CEO	Weighting	Target
1		Finance 1: Market Capitalization / PE Multiple	20%	
2		Finance 2: EBITDA%	15%	
3		Finance 3: Working Capital / Net Cash Flows	15%	
4		Customer 1: Internal Customer Survey / Employee Survey	15%	
5		Process 1: Cash Conversion Cycle	15%	
6		Process 2: # Initiatives Conducted to Increase Inter-departmental Communication	10%	
7		Learning & Growth 1: Implementation of the Balanced Scorecard	10%	

FIGURE 6.3 CEO Individual BSC

might find individual scorecards that have 20 objectives and 20+ measures. You would probably also find that they don't work! There's no surprise there. It's hard for an enterprise to deliver on 20 measures, so how can a single individual do so?

A good individual BSC identifies 5–7 measures, a combination of financial and non-financial. Figure 6.3 shows an example of an individual BSC for a CEO.

Of course, all individual objectives should be linked to the enterprise strategy. Here's a simple example: If the enterprise strategy is to maximize revenue from existing clients, what do you think the focus of the individual BSC for the sales head should be? A right answer could be as simple as: Grow revenues with current accounts.

Using the BSC to Formulate Strategy

This is probably the most important discussion in this chapter. A long time ago, I asked one of the creators of the BSC, a simple question: How come the BSC is not positioned as a framework to formulate strategy in addition to its execution? The key point in his response was that CEOs really want to feel like they own the strategy and that it is articulated in the way they prefer. There are also other management concepts that focus on the creation of strategy. Additionally, he pointed out, since the challenge is the execution, rather than the formulation, *why not just focus on the execution itself?*

There is, however, an alternate reality. The response above is based on a key assumption that most companies have a rock-solid strategy document that can be converted into a BSC for strategy execution. *That assumption is incorrect.* In many firms the strategy document is too blue sky, too budget- or market-research oriented, or *doesn't exist at all.*

This problem is especially rampant in the Middle East, and Asia, and also for mid-size firms globally. So it's not been unusual to find that when we are tasked with designing a BSC for a client, and we ask for a strategic plan, we don't get much. It almost forces us to turn the BSC program into a strategy formulation *and* execution program. There's nothing wrong with that, but it's better to be honest about what you are working toward. If you feel that your strategic planning document is not up to speed, then let the BSC program also be used to validate and enhance your strategy. End your strategy document with a financial, customer, process, organizational and IT strategy. That way, you can seamlessly bolt the BSC right onto your overall strategy. The purpose of this chapter has been to really give you a very quick introduction to the BSC. We are going to do a deep dive in a number of these areas but at least for now we aren't flying blind!

7

Challenges in Implementing the Balanced Scorecard Successfully

Time to Put on a Helmet!

For the past 20+ years, when I have worked on BSC programs, a typical question from a client is: *How many clients still have a successful BSC program running?* Most consultants or BSC coordinators would fudge an answer, but the honest reality is that at least 50 percent of them fail. That statistic is enough to scare anybody from using the BSC for strategic execution, but it is better to know the potholes before you start off on this journey. My opinion is that doing so will make sure you do an excellent job winding around the potholes, or better yet making sure they don't exist!

There are many challenges in implementing a BSC program successfully, and I have split them into three buckets: general, design, and implementation.

General Challenges

General challenges that firms face while implementing a BSC typically pertain to the existence of an actual, updated strategy, having the right sponsor with the right focus, and ultimately appointing the most appropriate coordinator to drive the implementation. The following are the biggest challenges in this area:

1. **You don't have the right sponsor.** For a BSC program to succeed, the ideal sponsor would be the CEO, but a c-level executive is required at the bare minimum for this role. If you don't have that, you are in trouble. Without c-suite sponsorship, there is a high likelihood that your resulting BSC will turn into a management information system (MIS) tool or a performance management system run by human resources (HR). These MIS and HR implementations may be misaligned with the enterprise strategy. It's what I call looking London, talking Tokyo!

2. **Your sponsor has a distracted mind.** I'm not trying to be mean here, but there are plenty of CEOs on the planet who have shorter attention spans than a hyperactive kid. Many CEOs will read a new book or learn a new management idea at a conference, and immediately want to implement it—that is, *until the next conference.* Soon the previous initiative is forgotten and there is a new flavor of the month. Remember, running the BSC is not like an initiative with a start and end date. It's a strategy deployment framework that is always on, very much like monthly budgeting process. The problem is that if the sponsor thinks that the BSC was a great initiative and now that it is done, it is time to move on, *the BSC program will fail.* What's important for the boss is important to the rest of us. That's human nature. Once the boss is not interested in something, everyone else also stops paying attention to it. In that case, you might as well bury it.

3. **You are missing a strategy.** As I indicated in the previous chapter, the BSC was designed to be an execution tool, not a formulation tool. It assumes that there is a strategy document in place, or at least the strategy is thought through so that it

can be validated and executed using the BSC. If you are missing that, there is no harm in combining a bit of strategy formulation at the start of the BSC program to ensure it succeeds. Otherwise, it will fail.

4. **You picked the wrong BSC coordinator.** The right BSC coordinator can make or break a project. The worse thing to do is to treat the BSC as a strategy audit tool and pick someone from internal audit. Let's be honest. Who wants to have an honest conversation with an internal audit person, who can only count the trees but can't see the forest?

Design Challenges

This is a big one. If you don't get the design right, you'll be stuck implementing the wrong strategy and driving down the wrong road. Here are the nine top pitfalls to avoid:

1. **Too many or too few objectives.** A good BSC design has about 20–25 objectives; that's five for each perspective. The more objectives you pick, the harder the strategy map becomes to read. This blurs the causal relationships between objectives. On the other hand, if you do not have enough objectives, it basically means you have missed 50 percent of your strategy. Good luck with that!

2. **The objectives are too verbose or too vague.** People sometimes get carried away with what they want to say in an objective. They make it so detailed that it is not readable. Others tend to be so blue sky and vague that the objectives are almost motherhood. The problem with that is, when you read it one month later, you will have forgotten what you were talking about and what specific area of strategy you wanted to focus on. Keep your objectives clear and concise. See Figure 7.1 for some examples of what works and what doesn't.

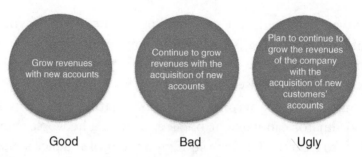

FIGURE 7.1   Good, Bad, and Ugly (Design Challenges)

3. **Too many measures.** The classic BSC design includes one lead and one lag measure per objective. (We will get to what this means later.) That means for 25 objectives you have 50 measures. My view is that this is great in theory, but way too much in practice. The human mind is not designed to respond to 50 measures at one time. Also, at any given time some will be on target and others off, which makes it difficult to figure out if you are in good shape or bad shape. The indicators go in both directions.

4. **The wrong measures.** The biggest problem with measurements is that it is an art and science. People select the wrong measures all the time and, even worse, they spin them to look good and hide a grim reality. It reminds me of a story I once heard about a Russian tractor factory that measured productivity in tons. The manufacturing head simply increased the weight of each tractor to show that productivity was up.

5. **Is the data available?** This is a big issue. It's great to select the most appropriate measures, but is the MIS system in place to track them? There's no question that it's important to track what needs to be measured rather than measuring what is easily available. However, if you design a BSC around measures that are not already collected, then you have to wait six months for the MIS to be put in place to track them. The BSC

is dead on arrival. By the time you have the data and start reporting the scorecard, it's too late to execute the plan. Be realistic about the data resources you have available.

6. **Wrong ownership of the objective.** We are going to talk about this at length in Chapter 10. The ownership of the objective has been given to the wrong person whose operational responsibility is not in the area of the objective's focus.

7. **Wrong target setting.** Too many stretch targets are set, so every time you report a BSC, you have too many reds on the board. What a de-motivator! Remember that only 3 or 4 objectives out of 25 should be stretches. Succeeding on those is enough to deliver a strategy. Don't overdo it.

8. **Poor initiative mapping.** Most executives don't understand the definition of an initiative or a project, and how it varies from standard operational responsibility. If you try to map the existing initiative list against the BSC objectives, you might have trouble. We will address this issue in Chapter 14.

9. **Cascaded design doesn't match the enterprise strategy.** If you want a strategy-focused organization, using the BSC cannot be limited to only those who have the keys to the executive washroom. The strategy has to flow through the organization using BSC cascades. Make sure the cascades align with the enterprise strategy. For example, if the enterprise strategy is to drive profits faster than revenue, the cascade strategy cannot be to grow revenue faster than profits.

Implementation Challenges

If you get the design right and you blow up the implementation, all you get is a nice BSC strategy map and design that, at best, you can frame on the wall like a piece of art. That wasn't the plan. The whole point of the BSC is to implement strategy, so follow it closely. Here are the seven biggest pitfalls to watch out for:

1. **It took too long to go live.** The design got done but then the BSC coordinator took time being a perfectionist and delayed the BSC launch. The problem is that human nature has a very short attention span. If you don't get something going within 60 days of completing the design, the momentum is lost.

2. **You are looking for 99.999 percent accuracy.** We selected a set of 30–40 measures. You could go crazy writing out the formula for each measure or trying to assess the accuracy of each one as if your life depended on it. That's the wrong idea. The purpose of having a measure is to ensure that we are driving the strategy in the right direction at approximately the right speed. That's all the accuracy we need.

3. **The data for many measures is not available.** The MIS system is weak, resulting in difficulty in pulling the data. We will talk about automation soon.

4. **The monthly meeting is not happening on time.** A typical BSC review is a monthly review. Due to hectic travel schedules, the meeting gets moved around. This is a bad idea and will cause the process to fall apart. The seventh of every month is a good standing date to do a review.

5. **The BSC coordinator has to defend the reds.** The meeting happens, and the BSC get reported. Guess what? It's a bad month; there are too many reds. The BSC coordinator is forced to defend them, even though that's not his job. The objective's owner should defend performance. The BSC coordinator is just a facilitator with good insights.

6. **Nothing happens.** The whole point of a BSC program is to observe the challenges in executing strategy, and react to them to drive change. If your BSC reveals issues, you need to address them immediately. Otherwise, nothing happens, and month

after month, you keep reporting the reds and not reacting to them. Then, the BSC program has failed.

7. **There are too many changes to the design.** This happens often. The BSC starts getting reported but at every meeting somebody tries to change the objectives, measures, or targets. That's okay for the first month or so before the design has stabilized, but after that, if you keep changing the design, there will be no consistent reference points left, and the scorecards will not reveal anything because comparing months will be like comparing apples to oranges.

If you can overcome these challenges, then there are happy days ahead, both for the organization and the shareholders.

Challenges in Balanced Scorecard Design

8

Designing the Strategy Map

Keep It Lite

Introduction

Talking about maps reminds me of a recent trip to London. I was riding in one of London's famous black cabs and the driver was complaining about how Uber has made life hard for London cabbies. Cab drivers need to spend over three years memorizing London street maps before they are allowed to drive a cab, it was a huge time investment but it kept competition low. Now, all these Uber drivers relying on Google Maps jumped in and snagged fares without having to spend three years studying. The new competition was driving the cabbies crazy.

This offers two great insights for us and business leaders around the world concerned with strategy. The first is that whatever technology you use, you need to have a map to find your way around your market. The same is true whether you are providing a taxi service or servicing customers around the world. The second insight is even more important. It's the idea that technology can be a great disrupter, and the person with a better, more dynamic Strategy Map can become competitive and very quickly threaten your business. *So, mapping your strategy correctly and having an excellent framework is critical to execution excellence. Let's talk about Strategy Maps.*

Design Methodology

Designing a Strategy Map for an organization should be easy, but it often is not. You might assume that if you simply read the strategy document carefully and takes good notes, the top 20–25 key strategic objectives will leap out of the pages for you to capture in a strategy map. Unfortunately, it's a bit harder than that. As we have discussed, in many organizations the strategy document does not capture the full strategy. Everything that is written may not be fully accurate and everything that is currently happening may not be written down. Developing a good understanding of a firm's strategy requires one to carefully read all internal and market-related documents, but also have frank and confidential one-on-one conversations with key members of the leadership team.

These one-on-one confidential conversations are critical. Most executives within an organization have a clear view of strategy, more than we have given them credit for so far. The problem is that nobody has listened to them intently or made an effort to put all the pieces of the puzzle together.

When the conversation is done by an internal executive (e.g., the strategy head), there is a possibility that the executives may speak up, but there is also a big chance that they may not be totally open about their views. This is especially true in Asian, Middle Eastern, and even some European markets, where speaking openly or criticizing the boss or the organization is not considered appropriate or professional. Often it's best to have a BSC specialist run the conversation. Of course, having a great conversation and being able to challenge some of the points being made depends on the BSC specialist who is directing the conversation.

It's important for this person—especially if he comes from outside the company—to have strong insights into the relevant financial, customer, process, organizational, and technology areas. This takes thorough preparation.

The conversations should aim to cover the person's views on the following issues:

- The overall strategy of the organization
- The strengths and weaknesses of the organization
- The positive and negative factors of the boss
- The positive and negative factors of professional peers
- The quality of their own team and its ability to deliver the strategy

As long as the executive is confident that the conversation is confidential, and that the person she is talking to is credible and knowledgeable, the conversation will flow and great insights can be obtained.

Once you have collated all the inputs from the conversation and has absorbed the insights from the documents, it's not hard to build a Strategy Map that does what Google Maps is doing for Uber drivers—and a lot of us nowadays.

After the one-on-one conversations are complete, it also helps to build the management team's consensus on the BSC program. After all these are the same executives who need to own the BSC and Strategy Map and its execution going forward.

Strategy Map Design Components

The traditional Strategy Map has four perspectives: financial, customer, process, and learning and growth. Each of these perspectives addresses unique business elements and topics. Figure 8.1 provides a template that gives you an idea about what each perspective includes.

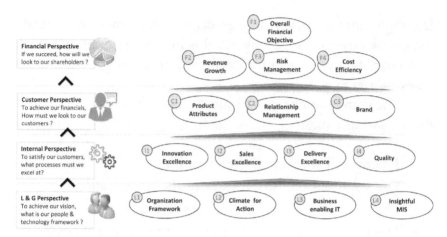

FIGURE 8.1   Generic Strategy Map

Financial Perspective

Let's face it. All businesses are in the business of making or managing money, so it's logical that the Financial Perspective sits at the top as the final endgame. This does move around when we design Strategy Maps for support functions or government organizations, where it's more about financial accountability but we will talk about that later in this chapter and also in Appendix A.

The overriding financial objective is aptly called F1. You find this by answering the question: *What's the financial endgame?* In my experience over the years, I see only three:

1. Grow revenue faster than profit.
2. Grow profit faster than revenue.
3. Forget about profit, let's just focus on maximizing market share.

You'd be amazed, but there are many CEOs who don't know which of these they want, or say they want all three at the same time. Making this decision takes total clarity because, at the end of the day, the F1 objective drives the rest of the strategy.

Sitting below F1 are, typically, 4 or 5 other financial objectives. I like to organize them by keeping revenue drivers on the left, risk-management objectives in the center, and cost/efficiency drivers on the right. Figure 8.1 reflects this and gives you a sense of what the generic strategy objectives should be, so when you document the detailed objectives, you haven't created an unbalanced scorecard by omitting any key area. For example, a financial strategy cannot be about only revenue growth; it also needs to cover risk and cost.

Customer Perspective

The next level is the Customer Perspective. The logic is clear. If you have a happy customer, you should fulfill the objectives in your financial strategy. Generally speaking, there is no real benefit to meeting customer expectations if it doesn't result in any short- or medium-term financial gain.

The question that most frequently arises during discussion of the Customer Perspective is: *If we do everything right in terms of processes, what are the key customer expectations we need to meet in order to accrue the financial benefits we are seeking?* Customer objectives are generally written from the customers' perspective and they tend to cover the following three key strategic areas:

1. Product and Service attributes, in terms of price, timely delivery, and cost.
2. Effective management of the customer relationship.
3. Success in meeting customers' brand expectations.

As in the Financial Perspective, these areas appear on the map in that order, from left to right.

Internal Perspective

This perspective focuses on the key process areas that an organization must excel at internally. Again, these are broken into five focus areas to keep it balanced:

1. Identifying opportunities
2. Innovation – developing products/services to meet those opportunities

3. Sales and marketing effectively to leverage those opportunities
4. Delivery excellence
5. Excellence in service or product quality

The topic of process excellence is vast, and so many books have been written about it. Companies spend big bucks to make sure they have the best process framework for their organization. Despite years of focusing on process, most organizations screw up regularly in this area. I believe the BSC, and specifically the Strategy Map, can play a very significant role in identifying and prioritizing the key process areas that you need to excel in order to drive strategy execution. Let me explain how.

The challenge of *real process transformation* when driving strategy is the ability to *prioritize* and determine which processes have a significant impact on reaching your strategic objectives. Besides the obvious 80/20 rule—20 percent of the processes result in 80 percent of the impact—my approach is to prioritize processes that drive performance. It includes, but is not limited to:

1. Processes that have a high cost per transaction
2. Processes that have a very high frequency
3. Processes that have a significant impact on customer satisfaction

If we use this approach and combine it with four or five of the internal perspective focus areas identified above, I think there is a real chance of ensuring that executing the strategy using the BSC is successful.

Learning and Growth Perspective

The Learning and Growth (L&G) perspective has always been a bit wordy, but it addresses how an organization can learn and grow from a human resources perspective, using technology as an enabler. The typical five areas that define L&G include:

1. Organizational framework, structure, and role definition
2. Organizational culture and climate for action

3. Performance and compensation orientation

4. Strong information technology (IT) backbone at the enterprise level

5. MIS that can drive strategy and provide insight

The essence of the L&G perspective is that an organization's people and technology drive processes. That, in turn, helps meet customer expectations, which helps meet the shareholders' financial expectation. It also emphasizes that *people are the foundation to a successful strategy of a firm.* I agree and disagree. I have seen too many examples of a company's progress being impacted due to an excessive focus on carrying the people within the organization. That is why I always say, *"People are important, but not at the cost of progress."* I know it sounds contrarian, but it actually highlights how important it is to have the right people on board. That might mean identifying the *wrong* people and helping them find where they'd be a better fit, allowing you to replace them with people who can better help you reach execution excellence.

Impact of Industry Customization and Support Functions on Strategy Map Design

Needless to say, the Strategy Map needs to be unique for your organization, and industry. Figures 8.2 and 8.3 provide a sample Strategy Map and Scorecard for a bank. While there are no generic Strategy Maps, Appendix A includes samples for a number of different industries: retail, telecom, manufacturing, real estate, hospitality, higher education, the public sector, oil and gas, fast food, and pharmaceuticals. The bottom line is there is no real difference in the perspectives the Strategy Map includes, however the design is influenced by the industry and whether it is for a support function or not.

Support functions do not often have a direct revenue-generating objective, but they have serious financial accountability.

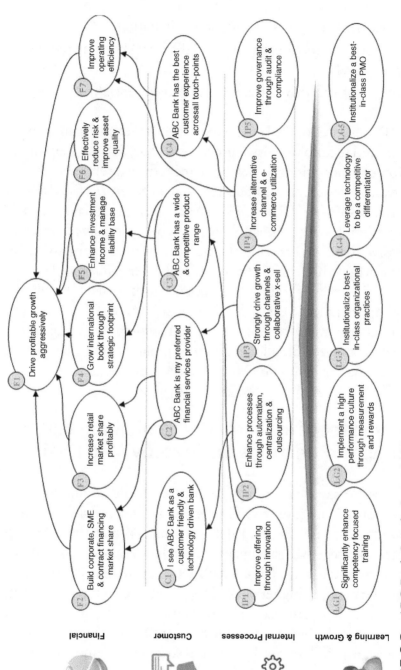

FIGURE 8.2 ABC Bank Sample Strategic Map

50

Obj #	Objective	#	Measure	Unit	Freq	Objective Owner	Month A	Month T	YTD A	YTD T
FINANCIAL										
F1	Drive profitable growth aggressively	1	Net Profit Growth	%	Q	CEO				
		2	ROE	%	Q	CEO				
		3	Share Price to Book Ratio	%	M					
F2	Build corporate , SME & contract financing market share	1	Non-funded Commission Income	USD	M	Head – Wholesale Banking				
		2	Corp. Book Market Share	%	M					
		3	SME Book Size	USD	M					
		4	Contract Fin. Book Size	USD	M					
F3	Increase retail market share profitably	1	Retail Book Market Share	%	M	Head – Retail Banking				
		2	Retail Revenue	USD	M					
		3	Fees & Commission Income	USD	M					
F4	Grow international book through strategic footprint	1	International Book Size	USD	M	Head – International Banking				
		2	Income from Int'l TF	USD	M					
F5	Enhance Investment Income & manage liability base	1	Investment Income	USD	M	Head – Treasury & Investments				
		2	Income from Proprietary Trading	USD	M					
		3	Cost of Funds	%	M					
F6	Effectively reduce risk & improve asset quality	1	NPL/Total Loans	%	M	Head – Risk Management				
		2	Operational Losses	USD	M					
F7	Improve operating efficiency	1	Operating Cost % of Total Revenue	%	Q	Head - Finance				
		2	Revenue/Employee	USD	Q					
CUSTOMER										
C1	I see ABC Bank as a customer friendly & technology driven bank	1	Customer Satisfaction Index	Score	H	Head - Ops. & Technology				
		2	eBanking Trans/Total	%	M					
C2	ABC Bank is my preferred financial services provider	1	X-Sell: No. of products per customer	Nos.	Y	Head – Marketing				
C3	ABC Bank has a wide & competitive product range	1	Revenue from New Products	USD	Y	Head – Retail Banking				
C4	ABC Bank has the best customer experience across all touch-points	1	Customer Satisfaction Index	Score	M	Head – Marketing				
		2	Customer Attrition	%	M					
PROCESS										
IP1	Improve offering through innovation	1	No. of products & services relaunched	Nos.	Q	Head - Marketing				
		2	Product Range Vs Regional Benchmark Index	Nos.	Q					
IP2	Enhance processes through automation, centralization & outsourcing	1	SLAs for key processes	Nos.	M	Head – Ops & Technology				
		2	Process Errors/Rework	%	M					
		3	Internal Customer Survey	Score	H					
		4	Operating Cost/Employee	USD	M					
IP3	Strongly drive growth through channels & collaborative x-sell	1	Branch RAG Performance	%	M	Head – Wholesale Banking				
		2	Sales/branch for all products	USD	M					
		3	X-Sell: No. of Retail Products per customer	Nos.	Q					
		4	Inter-department cross sell penetration	%	Q					
IP4	Increase alternative channel & e-commerce utilization	1	Internet Banking Trans/Total	%	Q	Head – Marketing				
		2	Call Centre Trans/Total	%	Q					
		3	ATMs/CDMs Trans/Total	%	Q					
IP5	Improve governance through audit & compliance	1	Internal Audit Ratings	Rating	Y	Head – Risk Management				
		2	Regulatory Audit Ratings	Rating	Y					
ORGANIZATIONAL & IT										
LG1	Significantly enhance competency focused training	1	Training days / Employee	Nos.	H	Head – HR				
		2	Utilization of e-learning	%	H					
		3	Senior Management Survey	Score	H					
LG2	Implement a high performance culture through measurement and rewards	1	Variable Compensation % of Total Salary Cost	%	Y	Head – HR				
		2	Number of Promotions	Nos.	Y					
LG3	Institutionalize best-in-class organizational practices	1	Employee Survey	Score	Y	Head – HR				
		2	HR Compliance Index	Score	Q					
LG4	Leverage Technology to be a competitive differentiator	1	KMS for Technology Projects	-	Y	Head – IT				
LG5	Institutionalize a best-in-class PMO	1	Senior Management Survey	Score	H	Head – Ops & Technology				
		2	KMS for Project Management Office	%	Y					

FIGURE 8.3 ABC Bank Sample Scorecard

Support functions include human resources (HR), information technology (IT), and finance, to name a few. Therefore, in the case of support functions, the top-most perspectives deal with customers, followed by financial accountability, process, and L&G. The logic is simple. In order to meet the expectations of internal and external customers, support functions need to be accountable for the funds allocated from either internal or external resources.

Strategy Map Design for Nonprofit and Government Organizations

The design principles for support functions also apply to nonprofit and government organizations, and, in many cases, nonprofit educational institutions. These are all entities that have financial accountability, but no revenue-generating accountability. Appendix A includes sample maps and scorecards for the public sector and higher education. You will notice that the stakeholder perspective is at the top of the Strategy Map, with financial accountability underneath it.

I hope that, at this stage, you are starting to feel a bit like the Uber driver with Google Maps—really confident about the direction of your strategy.

The Concept of the Linkage Model

One of the original terms used to describe a Strategy Map was a *strategic linkage model.* The logic was simple: Every strategic objective on the Strategy Map needs to have a positive cascading impact on the next level. In the strategy maps in Appendix A, the impact is indicated with arrows leading from one objective to another. In other words, strategic objectives do not stand alone, but just like everything on a map, need to be connected. While this sounds like an easy and obvious principle, actually plotting these connections on a Strategy Map can lead to confusion. Many

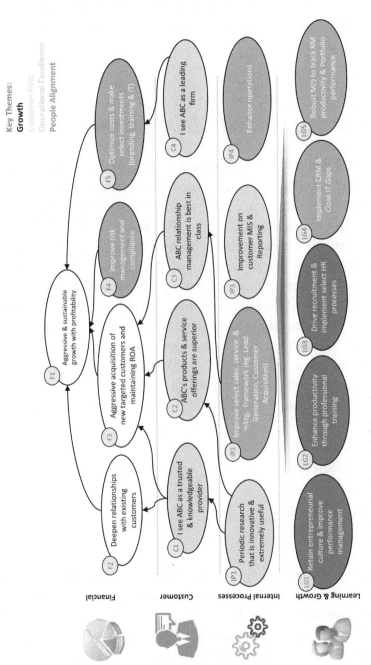

Key Themes:
Growth
Customer First
Operational Excellence
People Alignment

FIGURE 8.4 Theme-Based Lite Strategy Map

53

clients feel the map contains too many lines, and when that happens I dispense with the arrows. You are, however, welcome to stay with them.

Designing a Lite Version of a Strategy Map for Board Reporting: Strategic Themes

Very often, I will get a client request to design a lite version of a Strategy Map and BSC for board reporting. The reason is that the CEO wants to communicate progress on execution of strategy to the board, but doesn't have a framework to do so. The Strategy Map and BSC do a great job of achieving this. They identify the drivers delivering financial results and the progress that is being made on each of them. These lite tools are great to use in addition to budget documents because they give a good visualization of the big picture and how different strategic objectives work together.

At the same time, the board does not have the time or inclination to see a full 25-objective strategy map. In cases like these, I recommend converting a full Strategy Map into a lite version by focusing on the top four or five strategic themes, such as:

- Transformational growth
- Global expansion
- Customer excellence
- Cost optimization
- Internal change

Figure 8.4 highlights strategic themes from a full strategy map. You can index some measures for the top 4 or 5 themes, as we will discuss in Chapter 11.

Having a lite, theme-based Strategy Map is a great way to articulate the management team's success in executing the strategy to the board and other stakeholders.

9

Defining Objectives

The Wordsmith's Challenge

We are quite clear on what the design framework of a Strategy Map looks like. Let's now look at the issue of how people articulate their strategic objectives, and what are good and bad ways to do it.

The Bad Way

In articulating a strategic objective, the management team creates a long sentence, as in Figure 9.1. This happens often. Not only does it overflow from the bubble, but it also is very hard to see clearly. To make your map functional, you have to keep it simple.

However, do not make it too simple. Another problem is putting too little text in the objective bubbles. That's also bad because it is not descriptive enough to mean anything. Look at Figure 9.2. It could be a strategic objective from anyone's strategy map, as there is nothing unique about it. By the time you revisit this at the next monthly meeting, you will have forgotten the

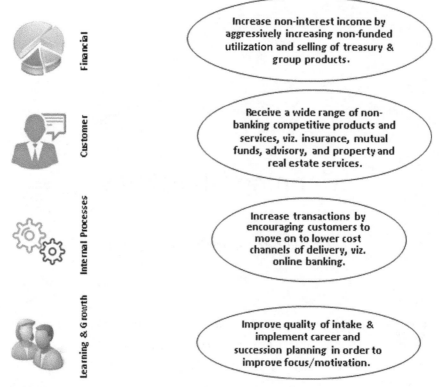

FIGURE 9.1 A Strategic Objective with Descriptions that Are Too Long

underlying discussion that drove the creation of that objective, and it's whole purpose will be lost.

The Good Way

The good way is to make it not too long and not too short. just right. Look at Figure 9.3 for an example. I guess I have made my point.

There is one other thing to keep in mind to create good objectives. Be very careful about the *intensity* of the objective

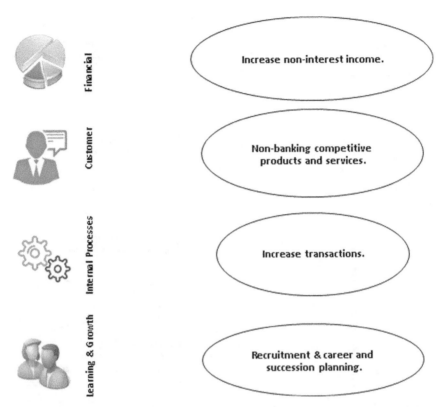

FIGURE 9.2 A Strategic Objective with Descriptions that Are Too Short

and ensure it states what you want to achieve. Sometimes management teams get carried away in a workshop, and will add the word *significant* to just about anything. For example, they want to "*Significantly exceed customer expectations.*" Consider the implications of this commitment. By adding the word *significant*, you have turned this objective into a stretch target. If your current customer satisfaction is 5 out of 10, significantly exceeding customer expectations means increasing that number to at least an 8 out of 10. That means you have to show a huge improvement. Do you have the wherewithal to make that happen? Do you have the resources to make that happen? Is it even

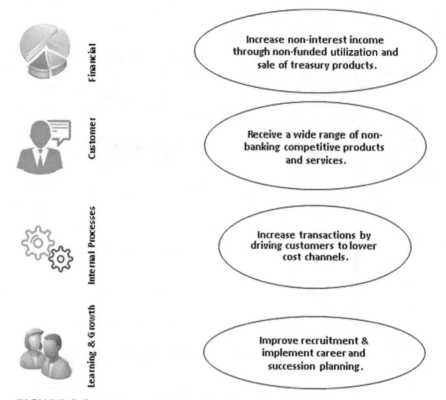

FIGURE 9.3   A Strategic Objective Done the Right Way

really necessary? Do your customers really expect it? Are they willing to pay for that level of service? Take it easy and don't get carried away. Commit to objectives that are both necessary and feasible.

Customer Objectives

In using the BSC to execute strategy, customer objectives are articulated differently than the other objectives because *they are written from a customer's perspective*. The logic is simple. If you do everything right in the coming year in terms of learning and

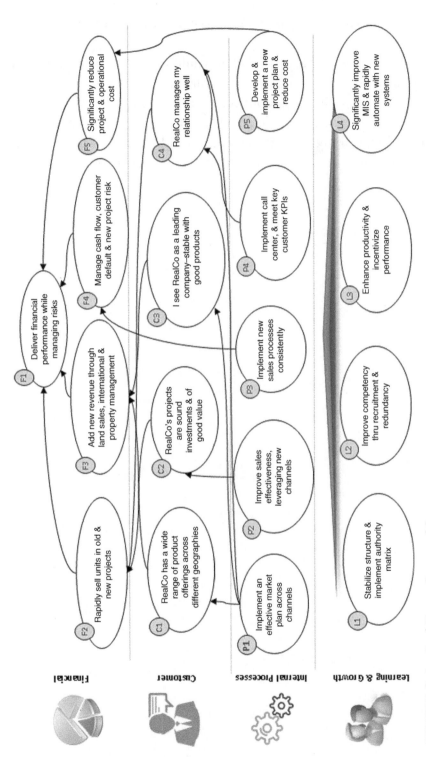

FIGURE 9.4 Real Estate Strategy Map

growth, and your processes, what would you like for customers to say in a survey about the organization. Keep in mind that customer experience is connected to financial objectives. Look at the Strategy Map in Figure 9.4 and you can see how this has been done. In my view, these areas would be the top five areas in any customer survey that one designs and executes.

10

Picking Owners

Four Executives Don't Run a Company

Who owns the formulation of a company's strategy and who owns the execution? These may seem like simple questions, but I can assure you confusion exists on these topics. To a large extent, the lack of clarity in answering these questions also contributes to the failure in designing a strategy that can work, and executing it successfully.

Owning the Formulation

We all agree that for an organization to succeed, its people need to be aligned and focused in one direction. As we endeavor to achieve that, an assumption is made that the strategy that is formulated needs to be bottom-up, not top-down. While that sounds very democratic (and in my view somewhat socialist), it's not the right way to approach strategy.

Here's the issue: As one moves down an organization, the roles and competencies become more operational and less strategic. That group is really focused on getting the job done, and preoccupied throughout the day with meeting customer expectations. When executives put a new idea on the table, the rest of the organization immediately thinks of how this new idea can be delivered through the existing operating framework and processes. If it can't, the red flags go up and the immediate response is that it can't be done because the existing processes or technology cannot handle it.

This perspective misses the whole point of developing a new, breakthrough strategy, which is to do things differently. Therefore, I am a strong believer that strategy needs to be formulated by those with the keys to the executive washroom. Even within this elite group, it's possible to find gaps in strategic thinking, which is why consultants exist—to bring in new ideas and facilitate their induction into organizations. There is no harm in getting some internal feedback from four levels below the CEO. The leadership team can use that information to make a strategic call and include input from the organization that they feel is relevant. From my standpoint, it's clear that *formulation is the prerogative of the leadership team. That's what they get paid to do.*

This doesn't absolve them of the responsibility to effectively communicate the strategy throughout the organization and facilitate alignment. Having a strong internal communication framework is key to do this, and this is where the Balanced Scorecard (BSC) plays the most effective role of communicating strategy through the organization and driving performance.

Owning the Execution

So far, it's quite clear that the top 25 objectives on a strategy map and BSC should be owned by the leadership team and the specific individuals who are operationally responsible for delivering the objectives. For example, a sales objective is owned by the head of sales. That person may rely on others within the organization to develop analysis to support understanding of specific, performance-related issues. With this assistance, the head of sales will fully understand the data and measures, and be able to lead a discussion on the topic in the monthly management meeting.

This should not be seen as generating additional work for the head of sales. Even if the BSC didn't exist, leaders should know what is actually going on. In fact, the BSC helps leadership teams develop a strong focus and understanding of some of their existing operational responsibilities.

There are situations when no one on the management team is qualified to own a BSC objective. In that case, the CEO can pick someone from the leadership team to own it. This could be an executive who is being groomed for the c suite, or simply a high-performing individual. One thing is clear—ownership of a strategic objective is not a task for junior-level executives or project managers, even those who oversee key strategic initiatives.

As we mentioned before, the CEO will own objective F1, the overriding financial objective, as well as other select objectives within the BSC. Don't worry that too many objectives will be loaded onto one executive. The math is simple: The BSC has 20–25 objectives, and a leadership team has about eight executives, which works out to three objectives per executive. That's quite manageable. It's important that every member of the executive committee owns at least one objective. If this doesn't work out clearly, you should wonder if the strategy map is comprehensive enough or, worse still, if the wrong people are on the executive committee. Every c-level executive should be capable of owning an objective.

How Does Ownership Really Work in a BSC Meeting?

Let's take a regular monthly performance review using the BSC. The Strategy Map and BSC are opened up for discussion. Anything that has gone red comes up for discussion first. The executive who owns the objective leads the discussion on that strategic objective and explains why the objective is behind target, providing supporting documents, if needed. Then, the whole management committee spends the next 30 minutes discussing the specific issue, and working to find a solution to the problem. Very often problems within an organization do not originate from one department. For example, lackluster sales may result from a delay in recruiting new sales executives or a failure of manufacturing to meet demand. While it's the responsibility of the owner of the strategic objective to deliver the objective, it is the collective responsibility of the management team to find a solution to the problem, and support the owner in meeting the objective on a timely basis.

BSC Ownership versus Individual Performance Measures

Another area of confusion is the difference between owning a strategic objective on a BSC to execute strategy, and individual performance measures (IPMs). We have thoroughly described the components of a strategic objective, so you have a clear understanding of that. Individual performance measures include key result areas (KRAs) and key performance indicators (KPIs) that track performance.

The Strategy Map and BSC are about identifying the top 20–25 objectives that the *organization* needs to focus on to deliver the strategy. This does not include every single strategic and operational objective that is running within an organization. Once the executive is back in the office, there are two responsibilities to cover:

1. Strategic objectives reflected in the BSC
2. Operational objectives that are part of their daily responsibilities

Figure 10.1 shows the two side by side so you can compare them. A combination of these strategic and operational objects are

Enterprise Performance Management System (BSC)

Obj. #		Objective	Objective Owner	#	Measure	Unit	Freq	Month Tgt	Month Act	YTD Tgt	YTD Act
	Financial										
F1		Aggressive profitable growth	CEO	1	Book Size	$M	M				
F2		Grow all business groups - special focus on Cards, Priority Banking, Title products	CEO	1	ROE	%	M				
				1	Growth from key areas	%	M				
F3		Business creation/Credit and strong compliance	CEO	1	TAT%	Index	M				
				2	% NPA	%	M				
				3	Audit Rating	Rating	Y				
	Customer										
C1		Significantly improve cost efficiencies	CEO	1	Cost/Income Ratio	%	M				
C2		Has the best customer experience across touch points	GM Retail, GM Corp	1	Customer feedback	Survey Score	Q				
C3		See ABC as a leading bank	CEO	1	Market share	%	Q				
	Internal Process										
IP1		ABC has effective technology, including best-in-class electronic banking	GM-IT	1	Electronic banking transactions/Total	No.	M				
IP2		Drive innovation especially products	Head - Marketing	1	Revenue from new products	$M	M				
IP3		Significantly improve sales engine	GM Retail	1	Revenue/Sales FTE	$M	M				
IP4		Optimize channel mix & synergies	CEO	1	Channel mix target eg. Branch/ATM/web/X-sell	%	M				
	Learning & Growth										
LG1		Monitor and improve service quality	Head - Credit	1	SAT Index (sales-marval-enc/mfit reqts)	Index	M				
LG2		Improve structure & productivity	CEO	1	Profit/employee	$M	M				
LG3		Create a pref. & businesse oriented culture	GM Corp Centre	1	New Perf. Management system deployment	%	HY				
LG4		Drive employee satisfaction	GM Corp Centre	1	Employee satisfaction survey	Survey Score	Q				
LG5		Significantly improve MIS	GM STO	1	Employee feedback	Survey Score	HY				
		Implement & leverage top 3 key systems	GM STO	1	Key milestones compliance	%	M				

Executive committee members share responsibility in the delivery of enterprise strategy using an EPM.

Individual Performance Measures (IPMs)

Position	% Wtg	KRA	Actual	Target
Head-Strategy Planning	40	Interest cost management		
	30	M&As completed in defined time frame		
	10	Cost management of projects		
	10	Cumulative time overrun		
	10	Completion of initiative/projects		

Individual performance is a combination of strategic/BSC and operational responsibilities measured using an IPM/KRA/MBO system aligned to BSC.

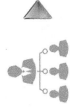

FIGURE 10.1 Boardroom to Office

65

Sr. No	Perspective	Manufacturing Head	Weightage	Target
1		Finance 1: Production	30-35%	
2		Finance 2: Conversion cost per unit	15-20%	
3		Customer 1: Number of product-related complaints	10-15%	
4		Internal Process 1: OEE %	10-15%	
5		Internal Process 2: Finished Good Inventory Aging > 7 days, WIP Aging > 48hrs	10-15%	
6		Learning & Growth 1: Employee costs as % of revenue	10-15%	

FIGURE 10.2   IPM Manufacturing Head

reflected in an executive's job description, are part of the KRAs (key result area) and also compensation reviews and bonus programs. Typically, I do not recommend using more than five to seven IPMs for each executive, and my preference is to use the BSC framework to ensure the IPMs are well balanced. Figure 10.2 shows one such example.

In conclusion, formulating and executing the strategy is the domain of the leadership team. That's what they get paid for. Confusing the issue, failing to provide the organization with an opportunity to provide selective input, or neglecting to communicate the strategy effectively to create alignment would be tremendous mistakes resulting in execution failure.

11

The Art of Measurement

Lead, Lag, and How Many Are Enough

Introduction

I have to start with a saying that is dated, but does the job: *What gets measured, get done.* It's as simple as that. Kids graduate from one grade level to another in a completely transparent and quantitative manner using a grading system, and we should hold ourselves to the same rigors especially because, as executives and consultants, we get paid to get the job done.

That being said, when it comes to measurement, there is a cultural divide that needs to be addressed. In many cultures, such as United States, Germany, and others, measurement is a well-understood and appreciated concept. In general, *measurement motivates.* That's also because organizational structures and roles have matured in terms of understanding, accountability is clearer, and compensation is often linked to performance.

In many parts of Asia and the Middle East, *measurement scares.* In these cultures, public face is important, so showing blemishes in public has a negative impact on professional and social status.

More importantly, even if you get past the cultural challenge, there are other organizational issues that hinder progress. If the structure is unclear, if roles and responsibilities are poorly defined, if competencies for each position are vague, then people will not be able to do their jobs effectively, even if they have the right skills and attitudes, and are willing to be measured and assessed. Therefore, even before we begin defining measures, it's a good idea to step back and ensure that the organizational framework is stable and clear, and to close any gaps. At the bare minimum, at least the executives who are going to be responsible for executing strategy using the Balanced Scorecard (BSC) framework must have clarity about their accountabilities and objectives so that this does not become an issue later.

Financial and Non-financial Measures

Here's another issue. While financial measurement is important, we have become obsessed with it. In my view, there are two reasons for this. The first is simply that financial measurement is easy. It's all about the numbers, the formulas are generally clear, and the management information systems (MIS) have been geared to address this space. More importantly, the value of an enterprise is primarily measured by its financial performance, which is obviously important. Additionally, executive compensation nowadays is driven by financial rather than non-financial performance. The problem with this approach is that in strategy execution, the non-financial drivers drive the financial performance. Therefore having a combination of financial and non-financial measures is key. This brings up the issue of lead and lag measures.

Lead and Lag Measures

While financial measures are important, one of the challenges in is that they tend to be *lag measures*. What does that mean?

In simple terms, a lag measure is computed after the event is over, so there isn't much you can do about it. For example, quarterly earnings are a lag measure. Once the quarter is over, there is nothing you can do about it. Compare that to something like the number of sales calls per day, a *lead measure*. The logic is simple. Traditional logic is that an increase in sales calls will lead to an increased likelihood of sales. Therefore the number of sales calls is a lead measure, and the resulting revenue is a lag measure. Got it? It's important that, if you are keen to successfully execute strategy, you have a good mix of lead and lag indicators.

Strategic versus Non-strategic Measures

Besides worrying about balancing lead and lag indicators, you need to ensure that the measures selected to deliver strategy are as strategic in nature as possible, and that most of them are not operational. Let me give you an example. If you were measuring the performance of a call center, you could choose from over 100 operational measures, but in my view there are only three strategic measures, as shown in Figure 11.1.

#	Measure	Description
1	Call Drop Rate	How many calls dropped before they got answered
2	80/20 Compliance	Were 80% of the calls answered in the first 20 seconds
3	First-Time Resolution	% of calls resolving the issue in the very first call

FIGURE 11.1 Strategic versus Nonstrategic Measures

If a call center is a critical part of fulfilling customer expectations, selecting the right strategic measures will do the job. Of course, you can index the above measures to create a single number assigning appropriate weights to each measure.

Financial Measures

As I indicated earlier, financial measurement is a well-recognized science, and because I don't consider myself to be an expert on the subject, I am not going to spend too much time talking about it. I do, however, want to make a few comments.

First, there is a group of general financial measures that are pretty standard across industries. These include numbers from profit and loss (P&L) statements, balance sheets, key ratios, and stock-price computations. These tend to be measures that are not industry specific.

Then there are measures that are specific to an industry. Understanding and using these measures to design a BSC to execute strategy is very important. Relying on generic measures is not going to get you anywhere. For example, the hospitality industry relies on average room rate (ARR) and the telecom industry uses average revenue per user (ARPU). In Appendix E, I have provided a laundry list of select measures across a range of industries that are used fairly often. I hope you find them useful.

Customer Measures

Getting the measures right in the customer space is both easy and difficult. There are lots of measures that measure customer service, experience, and processes, but these need to fit into the internal perspective on our Strategy Map and BSC. Remember, the customer perspective on a Strategy Map typically covers topics in the three areas as shown in Figure 11.2 and therefore needs measures to support the related objectives.

These are trickier than you might think. For example, product and service attributes could relate to a customer survey with the results that can be attributed to quality, time, or price, depending upon what we consider most important to the customer. Meeting brand expectations can happen in multiple ways—the most obvious being to simply ask the customer directly. Alternatively, external measures such as share of voice or share of mind can also be helpful.

When we talk about meeting relationship management expectations, there is an aspect of customer experience (CX) and customer relationship management (CRM), but it encompasses more than that. For example in retail banking, it could be about a bank's channel strategy, which channel is responsible for engaging with the client. It can also reflect what the competencies should be. This is often true in the wealth management space. The role of relationship management is done by private bankers, but are they expected to be competent in product knowledge or merely to provide what I call *concierge services*. In the manufacturing industry, CX and CRM ensure an organization is serving the right segment of the market, directly or through a third-party distribution channel.

#	Area
1	Meeting Product/Services Attributes (Quality, Time, Price)
2	Meeting Brand Expectations
3	Meeting Relationship Management Expectations

FIGURE 11.2 Customer Measures

So as you can see, customer measures are more strategic than the traditional operating measures that will sit in the internal perspective.

Internal Perspective

Measures in the internal perspective are about measuring ones success in executing key processes well, which will in turn help meet customer expectations, and ultimately financial goals. If you go back to the Strategy Map, the generic internal perspective objectives can fall into the categories shown in Figure 11.3.

Depending on the specific objectives selected in each of the areas, the measures could vary significantly. This is especially true as industry-specific measures really kick in during the internal perspective, and processes tend to be industry specific. You can find a range of industry-specific scorecards and maps in Appendix A.

#	Objective	Measure
1	Identifying market opportunities	New markets identified
2	Creating an offering	New products commercialized
3	Selling and marketing the offering	Channel mix
4	Delivering the offering	On-time delivery index
5	Ensuring product & service quality	Error rate

FIGURE 11.3   Internal Perspective Measures

Learning and Growth Measures

Learning and growth (L&G) measures are interesting. One of the biggest complaints about human resources (HR) is that the value they add to businesses is not always very clear. While their key objective is to help create a performance-driven organization, they are not willing to be held accountable for their own performance. A simple example given to me is the delay in recruiting high-quality resources.

Nonetheless, the BSC is a good starting point to get HR accountable in executing strategy followed by a full HR Scorecard. A few typical HR objectives and measures are shown in Figure 11.4.

As you can see, HR measures tend to be less industry specific.

On the information technology (IT) side of the L&G perspective, the focus is on having the right IT framework to drive informed decision making and run the enterprise. It is not about an enterprise's core manufacturing IT systems or bank systems. These should be covered in the internal perspective. Typical objectives and classic measures for IT are shown in Figure 11.5.

#	Objective	Measure
1	Right structure & role clarity	KMS- Key milestones met
2	Strong competencies	% organization meeting competency requirements
3	Performance-driven culture	% compensation related to performance
4	Right headcount	People cost/total cost

FIGURE 11.4 Learning and Growth Measures

#	Objective	Measure
1	Fact-based decision making	MIS quality index
2	Mobile organization	% of transactions mobile enabled
3	Technology-driven enterprise	IT expenses as % of total expense

FIGURE 11.5   IT Objectives and Measures

Measurement Formulas

Measures are not as simple as they can often appear. Every one has a formula, and this can be the source of argument during performance and BSC reviews. In fact, often the biggest arguments during BSC reviews occur when the number on the board is incorrect. When this happens, it doesn't mean the data was incorrect, but that people made different assumptions about the formula, so they get different numbers.

Here's an example. For a telecom company, the number of subscribers could mean two things. From the finance perspective, it could be the number of subscribers who receive invoices. From the network perspective, it could be the number of live subscribers on the switch. There are lots of examples like this, but I think the point is very clear. Every measure must have a clear formula that is agreed upon and used consistently for every BSC reporting—and throughout the organization, if possible. You can't change it every month because doing so makes it impossible to track progress. You should also keep track of the formulae in a designated document so people can refer to it in case they forget them.

While I recommend keeping your formulae consistent form month to month, they do need to be reviewed periodically to ensure no rational changes are required. Here's another example: If revenue is a combination of the revenue of five divisions of a company, and a new sixth division has been activated, then obviously the revenue measure must be updated to reflect this. In your monthly meetings, it's a good idea to discuss these types of changes so you always have the best possible data.

Data Sources

Having a measure and a formula isn't enough to get you started. You need to find the data. This is the kind of problem that gives people headaches, and it has long been a problem with strategic measures. Remember: *Information is power, so sometimes it is hidden.* Tracking down the right data sources could be as hard as finding Mackenna's gold!

This is the reason IT organizations have grown over the years, along with their budgets. While they support the overall organization and improve the customer experience, their role is not commensurate with the level of investment made in IT systems. I know one bank that has 42 different systems feeding data to its branch. A typical bank may also have 25 key system categories at its core, each one shooting out its own version of data. Companies that have invested billions of dollars in systems, applications, and products (SAP) find that they still don't have data clarity because certain manual and spreadsheet records are still in place. *Measures for the number of customers could come out of the enterprise resource planning (ERP) system or the CRM system as well.* You get the picture. Ambiguity about data sources can wreak havoc on BSC measures.

It's, therefore, very important that once the measurement formula is determined, the data source is also identified. Ideally, the source should be as close to the raw data as possible because this increases the likelihood that it will be the most accurate. For example, I would never trust the sales organization to supply a count of the number of customers. That needs to come out of the financial system, which can clearly see the number of customers who have been invoiced, assuming that's the established definition.

Every measure has a corresponding formula, therefore in addition to finding data sources, the calculation for every month also needs to be automated so that the numbers are consistent month to month.

What about Missing Data Sources?

Sometimes a great formula is put together but the data doesn't exist. Here's a simple example: If the measure is *customer satisfaction* but you have never conducted a customer satisfaction survey, you obviously are not going to have the appropriate data. That means that a process has to be put into place to start conducting the surveys and capturing the data. Implementing a new process at that scale could take time. That is why it's good to look for a *proxy measure* to make up for this temporary gap. This ensures there aren't too many blanks in reported performance. A proxy for *customer satisfaction* could be *number of complaints received* or *number of repeat customers*.

How Many Are Enough?

This is the last section in this chapter, but it is an important one. The traditional BSC design recommends around 50 measures, basically one lead and one lag measure per objective. If you design a BSC with 20 objectives, you are dealing with 40 measurements. I'm exhausted just thinking about it!

The first issue with this is that most organizations still struggle on the MIS side. This has improved with business intelligence solutions, but there are still some challenges. BSC is not about what is currently getting measured, but what needs to be measured, whereas MIS focuses on your existing data practices. Often the measures that are the most difficult don't really get measured. If you design a BSC with 40 measures, there is a high likelihood that at least 10–15 of them are not currently being measured in the right way. By the time the right systems get going, a quarter or two may have passed. This delay will result in an incomplete scorecard on Day 1, and interest may be soon lost.

The more important issue is that the human mind finds it hard to process what 40 measures mean in terms of performance. If you put up a dashboard with 40 measures and 10–15 are red, there will be confusion about what's going on. Are you doing well or poorly? It's a mixed bag. Management teams can cherry-pick numbers to use the information to support what they want to see in a particular situation. For example, new customer acquisition numbers may be down, but revenues may be up because they are inflated by a large, one-time order.

I understand the benefit of having a lead and lag measure for each objective, but my general recommendation to clients is to start with *a default position of one measure per objective*, with a maximum of 25. Once the organization shows maturity and capability in handling a larger number of measures, it may be time to expand the scorecard.

For those organizations or firms that are very number driven and lose interest without a ton of numbers, I recommend *indexing a few measures* together into a single indicator to keep the score-card manageable. Of course indexing is a science, and simple averages will not do. You need to understand how to weigh your components to get it statistically right.

12

Units and Frequency of Measurement

Stay Honest

By now you know that we are moving from the left of the Balanced Scorecard (BSC) to right, addressing the various objectives. We agree that in order to succeed in delivering a strategy, ownership of objectives and the appropriate measures are important. But they're not enough.

Effective measurement is not only about the type of measure, but also the units and frequency of measurement (Figure 12.1). Those three elements combined give you a real indication of the health of the objective that is being tracked for execution. It's no different than when you take your temperature when you are sick. Your measure is temperature, the unit is Fahrenheit or Celsius (depending on where you are from), and the frequency is every three hours (or how ever often your doctor recommends you take your temperature).

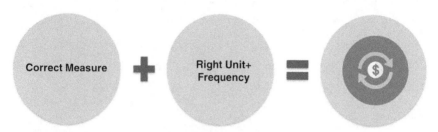

FIGURE 12.1   The Components of Effective Measurement

Units of Measurement

The idea here is not to educate you on the different units of measurement. You will know the general ones, and every business will have its own unique set. What's important is picking the *right* units of measurement so you get the strategic benefit you are seeking.

One common error is actual measurement versus a percentage. Let me give you a simple example. If a bank is planning to aggressively cross-sell credit cards to its deposit customers, one attempt to measure performance could be number of active credit cards. Lets say the actual number is 1 million. Somebody who looks at that number may immediately react and say it looks pretty good. However, if the total number of deposit customers is 5 million, then 1 million is not a great number. The preferred measure in this situation is *the percentage of the bank's customers who have a credit card*. Sometimes using incorrect measurements can even be intentional to hide weak performance.

It's important that the CEO or the head of the business unit responsible for that objective validate the measure, as the number will affect the tracking of strategy execution on a month-to-month basis going forward.

Key Milestone Indicators (KMS)

Sometimes there is a strategic project that is so important that you don't want to track its success with the other strategic projects.

You might consider it to be as important as a key strategy objective of the enterprise. An example of a project of this nature is *successful merger integration.* Suppose a firm has just bought another firm. The buyer spent a significant amount of money, so it is critical that integration is complete within six months of the purchase. Because the integration will impact strategy, I do not recommend tracking this as a typical project. Instead, I would add it as one of the firm's top 20–25 strategic objectives. The unit of measure would be Key Milestones (KMS) met, that let you know whether you are on track as far as your project milestones are concerned. So if the integration project has 10 milestones and 7 have been achieved, the indicator would be 7, or 70%, if you prefer.

Decimals

It's a small thing, but treatment of decimals can be irritating at times. I've seen BSCs that say the number of sales calls per day was 22.345. *Somebody is letting Excel control our common sense.* Sales calls either happen or they don't, so there is no question of decimals in this case. And don't even get me started about using three decimal places! Even God isn't that precise! Keep the numbers as simple as possible—preferably without any decimals. It's also a good idea configure the units so that there aren't *n* number of zeroes that pop up after the decimal point.

Frequency of Measurement

While decimals are a hygiene factor, the frequency of measurement is material. The purpose of using a BSC is to ensure your strategy is being executed in a timely fashion. If the frequency of measurement is incorrect, or too infrequent, then by the time you find out things are going wrong, it may be too late to change course.

Since traditional BSC strategy reviews are monthly, (*nothing wrong with that*) the typical frequency of measurement is also monthly. All *financial* measurement is monthly, which is already a common practice. All *customer* measurement, other than a potential customer satisfaction survey, should also be monthly. Following the pattern, all *process* measurements should be monthly. This should not be an issue at all, as generally speaking processes tend to get measured at a very high frequency. The *learning and growth* (*L&G*) measurement frequency, depending on the measure, will likely be quarterly or semi-annually. Examples include competency assessment, employee satisfaction surveys, IT satisfaction index, and so on.

In conclusion, executing strategy requires a solid understanding of the art and science of measurement and its various components, including type, unit, formula, data source, and frequency. When these are nicely aligned, your strategy will drive your business!

13

Target Setting

Actionable or Aspirational?

E xecuting strategy requires us to set financial and non-financial targets. Without knowing your target you can't get anywhere, let alone execute a strategy. So we don't really have an option here. (There are some exceptions, but I will get to those later.)

Target Intensity

Target intensity is a function of how aggressively you want to focus on the area. There are generally three levels of target intensity, as shown in Figure 13.1:

1. Realistic Targets
2. Aggressive Targets
3. Aspirational Targets

Realistic targets are those we feel pretty confident about achieving and know how to meet. In some cases we may not even need any significant resource augmentation, in terms of

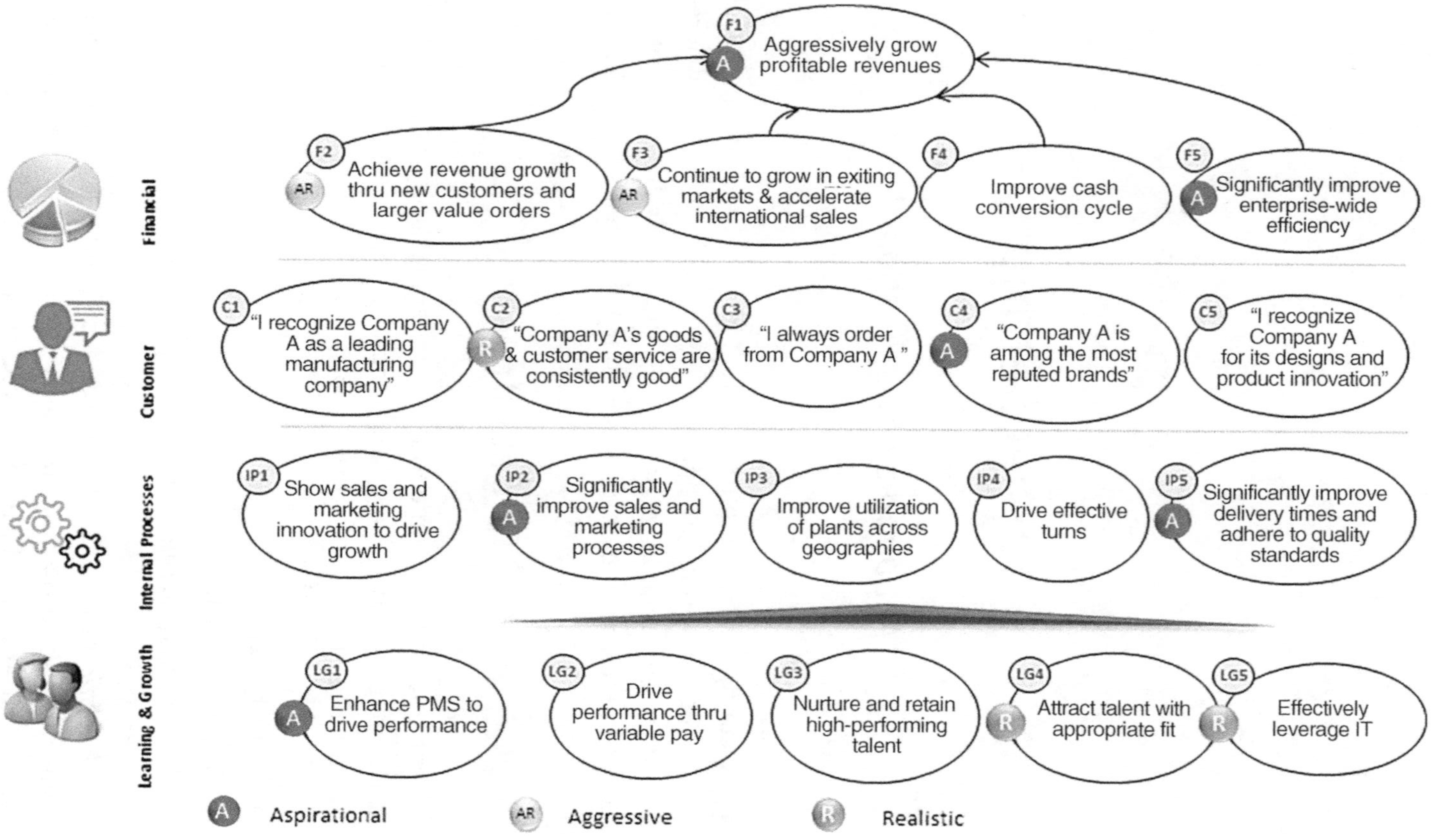

FIGURE 13.1 Target Intensity

Financial

Customer

Internal Processes

Learning & Growth

F1 Aggressively grow profitable revenues (A)
F2 Achieve revenue growth thru new customers and larger value orders (AR)
F3 Continue to grow in exiting markets & accelerate international sales (AR)
F4 Improve cash conversion cycle
F5 Significantly improve enterprise-wide efficiency (A)

C1 "I recognize Company A as a leading manufacturing company"
C2 "Company A's goods & customer service are consistently good" (R)
C3 "I always order from Company A"
C4 "Company A is among the most reputed brands" (A)
C5 "I recognize Company A for its designs and product innovation"

IP1 Show sales and marketing innovation to drive growth
IP2 Significantly improve sales and marketing processes (A)
IP3 Improve utilization of plants across geographies
IP4 Drive effective turns
IP5 Significantly improve delivery times and adhere to quality standards (A)

LG1 Enhance PMS to drive performance (A)
LG2 Drive performance thru variable pay
LG3 Nurture and retain high-performing talent
LG4 Attract talent with appropriate fit (R)
LG5 Effectively leverage IT (R)

(A) Aspirational   (AR) Aggressive   (R) Realistic

84

people or capital or technology. Here's an example: Last year, the employee satisfaction index was 5/10. This year we are going to play it safe and set the target at 6/10 because we don't plan to make any investments in staff engagement and, to be honest, we may even fire a few a people, which will not help the employee satisfaction number in this index.

Aggressive targets are those that are going to take a push. We know how to get there, but it's going to take a lot of effort. Aggressive targets may require some investments in people, capital, or technology. Here's an example: We are planning to grow sales by 30 percent while the market is growing at 10 percent. The only way to do it is to increase the size of the sales force by 40 percent, which will require a significant increase in headcount.

Aspirational targets are what dreams are made of. But if they show up in your BSC and become part of your strategy execution, *the dream needs to become a reality.* In these cases, existing processes may not be sufficient to deliver aspirational targets; some form of people, capital, or technology investment will definitely be needed. Here's an example: We are planning to double our revenues, but we don't know how we will get there with our existing business. An acquisition may be the best option in this case.

How Many Targets to Set of Each Kind?

I've talked about it before, but I am going to say it again: Executives get carried away, setting too many aggressive targets without realizing the consequences. Then, they complain when they don't reach them. There is a calm, calculated method for determining how many targets you should set in the three intensity levels.

Print out a copy of the strategy map, put it on your desk, close your door, and give yourself some time to think. Look at the endgame. Then look at all the objectives on the map. Now think about the four to six objectives that need to be really aggressive to make things happen this year. They should not all be in the same perspective (e.g. Financial). As I can't see your map, I can't say much more, except that you should make sure there is sound logic behind choosing your aggressive targets. Next, look for the two or three targets that need to be aspirational, then balance these choices with realistic targets. Once again, have a clear logic to assigning each category of targets.

A good way to guide you through the process is to carefully read the wording in each objective. As long as you have been disciplined about the language you use, you will find objectives in your Strategy Map that use the word *significant*. That word can clue you in to which are the aggressive or aspirational targets.

Take a look back at Figure 13.1 to see the intensity levels we assigned to the different objectives.

Target-Setting Benchmarks

Once we have figured out which of our targets should be realistic, aggressive, and aspirational, we need to determine how high should these targets be and what would be a good benchmark to compare our performance to. There are three main approaches, as shown in Figure 13.2.

#	Approaches
1	Looking at past performance
2	Looking at an internal benchmark
3	Looking at an external benchmark

FIGURE 13.2   Target Setting Benchmarks

The first option, looking at past performance, is the most common approach. Look at last year's numbers and pick a growth number for the coming year. For example, if revenue growth for the past three years was 10 percent per year, let's set this year's target at 15 percent, then come up with a plan to reach it.

The second option of looking at internal benchmarks is actually quite interesting and does not happen as often as it should. Let me explain. In a retail business, for example, you may have 100 stores. Typically these are categorized by performance, into three levels: A, B, and C. Now, we are keen to have the B-level stores do better. One way to push them to do so is to give them examples of competitors. That is quite logical, however management teams often resist this, giving excuses why this may not be valid, for example the processes of competitors may be more automated. My general recommended approach is therefore to use the achievements of the A-level stores as targets for the B and C performers. Surely, this may mean that they will have to set aggressive targets for themselves, and that may require additional capital, people, or performance bonuses. Those decisions can be made in a separate discussion about how to reach the targets. This is one example of how an internal benchmark can be used to set targets.

The third option, looking at external benchmarks, is used quite often. Let's return to our retail example. One way to encourage B and C branches is to provide examples of what competitors are doing. It's a reasonable approach, but management teams often resist, because a competitor's processes or systems may be different. As I indicated earlier, one may get a fair amount of resistance with this approach as no two companies are the same.

For management teams, there is always an excuse for why a particular benchmark cannot be used. At a strategic level, that argument is flawed. By that logic, the concept of valuing companies by comparing them with other firms in the same category, would not be valid. Even management teams must admit that the underlying logic in valuing companies on the basis of "comps" is the same as using external benchmarks. In my view, the benchmark valuation of a firm compared to another in the same industry is a validation of the principle of external benchmarking. If it works for the valuation of companies, I don't see why it would not work for other external benchmarks that are needed. Of course, we need to be intelligent about our selection of benchmarks. For example, you would not compare a large cap to a mid-cap for valuation purposes, unless you were trying to be aspirational.

Target Calculation

Calculating a target, especially an aggressive one, can sometimes get a bit complicated. Suppose your typical annual target was 20 percent growth, but this year, you've set it at 30 percent. Then, when you look at all your product lines or divisions, you realize that no matter what you do, you can't get their number past 22 percent. How do you bridge the resulting 8 percent gap? It's an interesting strategic challenge.

If the gap comes from a manufacturing capacity challenge, it could mean outsourcing manufacturing. If the gap results from a market opportunity gap, the solution could be contract manufacturing for another brand, or launching in a new market. It could even mean an acquisition. The key point I want to make is that *even the target-setting approach could result in some strategic decisions being made and executed.* It's not just tallying up rows and columns!

14

Initiative Alignment

Are You Overrun with Projects?

Companies have hundreds of projects and initiatives running all the time, consuming resources, all with the hope that they will help drive performance and execute strategy. The sad reality is that some do and most don't.

In the past 30 years, none of the hundreds of clients I've worked with could provide me with a list of existing projects running across the organization. Even eight weeks into the program, it is often uncertain if we have a complete list. Some overlooked project is always coming out of the woodwork, something we come across in some document, or something someone mentions in a conversation. Projects are supposed to drive strategy, *but nobody ever knows how many projects are running.*

It gets even better—or worse. When you try to track down a particular project manager, half the time you can't find the right person—if you can find anyone at all. If you are lucky enough to come across the right person and ask them about the project objective, don't be surprised if you don't get the correct answer. This means that many project managers are not even sure *why* they are doing a project.

It's grim news, but I know one thing for sure. The confusion is definitely keeping many people employed for a seriously long time. If you ask these project managers what they do for a living and what value do they add to the organization, they will tell you that they are delivering a project whose value they don't even know.

Initiative alignment won't fix the whole problem, but it will get you started. Do your best to take an inventory of all projects running in the enterprise. Aggregate them by functional area (e.g., finance, products, manufacturing, sales, marketing, sourcing, human resources, and technology), so you know how many projects are running and investment for each one. That alone will be an eye opener.

There are three steps to initiative prioritization, as shown in Figure 14.1.

Next, take the projects and map them against the strategic objectives in your BSC. You will be able to immediately identify which projects support which objectives, and which are orphans. It can help you consolidate, focus, and eliminate. Similar projects can be integrated. Too many in the same area can also be eliminated. New projects can be identified for unsupported

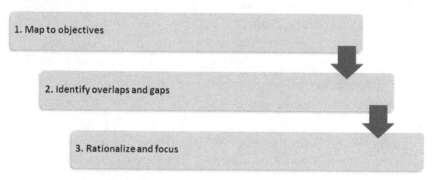

FIGURE 14.1   Initiative Prioritization

objectives. Doing this right can bring instant benefit to an organization. Even if you don't get any short-term financial value from using the BSC to execute strategy, I guarantee you will shave 30 percent off your existing project costs due to the process of initiative alignment.

15

Designing Cascades

Top Down or Bottom Up

Introduction

The Balanced Scorecard (BSC) has been designed to help execute strategy and drive enterprise performance. It would be foolish to assume that simply designing the corporate/enterprise-level BSC with a strong communication strategy and the support of 10 extremely capable members of an executive committee would be able to ensure the results we are seeking. The story does not end with the successful design and implementation of a corporate BSC; that's where it *begins*.

It is possible to design cascaded BSCs all the way from the top, down to a small department within a corporation. Let's first try to get at least one level below the enterprise BSC to the functional or business-unit level (Figure 15.1).

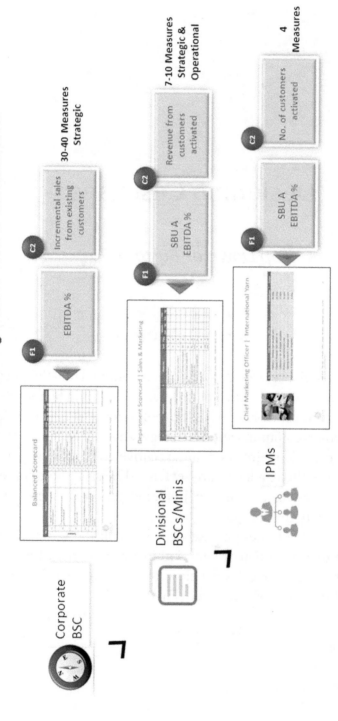

FIGURE 15.1 Cascade Flow

The Next Level Cascade: Functional Organization

The next level of a BSC cascade is really a function of the structure of the organization. For example, if an enterprise has a traditional functional structure, the next-level cascades will be for sales, marketing, manufacturing, quality, human resources (HR), finance, information technology (IT), legal, and so on. Some of these functions generate revenue, while others provide support and require financial accountability.

Let's take the sales BSC, for example. Clearly, this is a revenue-generating BSC, so the top perspective will be financial. However, the objectives, and the scorecard will need to align to the enterprise BSC. Therefore, it is very important to design an enterprise BSC before designing the cascaded BSC except if you have a very clear understanding of what the enterprise-level objectives and strategy are.

If the enterprise-level strategy is maximization of revenue from existing customers, then the sales BSC must also be aligned to this *objective*, and the related objectives must be aligned. If the sales BSC focuses primarily on acquiring new customers, then we know we do not have an alignment between the two BSCs, resulting in confusion and, potentially, a failed execution.

It's important to understand, when designing the objectives of a cascaded BSC, that some of them could be similar to the enterprise BSC if they make sense within that function, but most are likely to be new objectives, specific to the functioning of that department. For example, the process objectives most likely focus on delivering sales-related financial objectives, while learning and growth (L&G) objectives would focus primarily on the sales organization. It's important to remember that when we travel down through an organization, the roles and actions become more operational, so don't be surprised if some of the objectives seem more tactical than strategic.

Since this is a cascaded sales BSC, the head of sales will *own* objective F1. A large number of objectives for the Sales BSC will exist within the sales organization, but it is also likely that some of them could be owned by the relevant departments that support them. For example, a sales BSC could contain marketing objectives that the marketing department needs to own. Similarly, the sales BSC could include HR objectives that are owned by the HR department. However, *the overall success in delivering a cascaded sales BSC belongs to the sales organization.*

Some of the *measures* in a BSC cascade could match those in the enterprise BSC, but again this depends on the more operational objectives on the sales BSC. Those that are very specific to the cascade will require new measures to be defined. A good example would be *sales by channel.* This may not be an objective in the corporate BSC, but understanding the sales-channel mix could be critical from a sales strategy perspective.

The *targets* would definitely need to be aligned to the overall enterprise BSC. The numbers need to all be aligned and the formulas need to work. The enterprise's aspirational targets, which may not necessarily be built on a complex formula but rather on an aspiration, need to be reflected at the cascaded level. For example, if we set 9/10 as an enterprise target for customer experience, the cascaded BSC should also reflect that.

Project alignment is another important attribute of cascaded BSCs. At the enterprise level this is focused on the most strategic projects; however there are a number of projects executed at a departmental level to achieve the objectives on the cascaded BSC. That being said, it's possible that the same project is tracked at the enterprise and department levels, if the supported objective is shared.

Multi-divisional Structures and Cascades

It's quite common for organizations to have a multi-divisional or multi-company structure with a shared-services model. For example, a company could have a textile division, a yarn division, and a paper division. In such a situation, each division's BSC would, in many respects, look like an enterprise-level BSC. However, it is important to note that the objectives in a divisional-level cascade must align with those in the enterprise BSC. In a shared-services model, the L&G perspective of the cascaded BSC needs to be carefully designed, as there could be a shared-services unit that has part of the HR and IT functions embedded in it. If this were the case, the HR and IT objectives in the divisional BSC could be actually owned by the shared-services unit.

It's important to note that for a multi-divisional firm, the objectives and measures in the enterprise-level Strategy Map and BSC could have the look and feel of a *portfolio management strategy* similar to a conglomerate or a private equity fund. Let me explain.

When there is a portfolio of businesses, it is normal for some to be revenue drivers and others to be profit drivers, some to create more risk, some to require more capital, and some to have different cost efficiencies. A combination of all of these factors will drive F1, the *overall financial objective*. Therefore, it would not be unusual for an F1 objective in a multi-divisional company or conglomerate to reflect objectives oriented toward a shareholder expectation rather than just revenue, profits, or market share. Good examples of these types of objectives include:

- Drive enterprise value.
- Drive stock performance.
- Drive return on capital employed (ROCE).

Similarly, the objectives in the Customer, Process, and L&G Perspectives at the enterprise level would reflect a portfolio of businesses. The *customer* objectives could be more about the group's brand positioning and approach to customer relationship management (CRM). The *process* objectives could focus on mergers and acquisitions (M&A) to drive growth and leveraging sales, marketing, and manufacturing assets across businesses. The same approach would apply to the *L&G* Perspective.

16

Aligning Individual and Enterprise Performance

Unlocking Human Capital

Introduction

Over the years, as the Balanced Scorecard (BSC) has been embraced by the human resources department (HR), the framework has been used to more actively drive individual performance. Right now, there are hundreds of companies using what are called Individual Balanced Scorecards to drive employee performance. While the intention is good, the designs tend to be bad. Here's why.

Overenthusiastic HR professionals and consultants have taken a full BSC design meant for an enterprise and applied it to individual employees. Consider this: Normally, a BSC for a retail banking enterprise would be owned by the entire leadership team of about 10 people. It would have 30 measures and 20 objectives. So, what happens if the HR head uses that enterprise BSC to assess the individual performance of the head of retail banking? Someone's going to get a pretty rigorous annual review!

My question is simple. If an organization finds it difficult to deliver on 30 targets or 20 objectives, how could a single individual be able to do that? Some HR officers have gone one step further and connected the individual's annual review framework, which includes promotion and compensation reviews, to this major mistake. I have seen some of the most competent HR teams at major global banks do exactly that, so nothing surprises me anymore.

The Right Way

There is a right way to implement individual scorecards, but first we must understand the concept and application. The BSC is designed to help execute strategy and drive enterprise performance. As we've discussed, once a month the executive committee sits in the conference room and reviews the enterprise's performance. The objectives and measures in an enterprise BSC are strategic in nature; they do not intend to cover and track every activity within an organization. Instead, they focus on strategic objectives that are underperforming and the measures that help deliver on those underperforming objectives. That's what a regular BSC is meant to do. (See Figure 16.1.)

When the executives finish their meeting and go back into their offices, they return to fulfill their daily job descriptions. Their day-to-day roles include a combination of strategic and operational responsibility, but that operational responsibility is not reflected in any Strategy Map or BSC.

During the annual review process, shouldn't executives be reviewed on how they performed vis-à-vis their job description, which is a combination of strategic and operational responsibilities?

#	Area
1	Alignment with corporate and divisional BSCs
2	Alignment with structure
3	Right mix between financial and non-financial measures
4	Right mix between leadership and operational measures
5	Alignment with role profiles
6	All measurements are within person's direct control
7	No more than 4-6 measures per position

FIGURE 16.1 Right Way of Designing Individual Performance Measures

Measures

That being said, I still believe adapting the BSC framework to measure individual performance can be successful. The first step in this process is to establish appropriate measures, what I like to call *individual performance measures (IPMs)*. To begin, I typically pick a total of five to seven measures across the four BSC perspectives, and assign a weight to each one. (See Figure 16.2.)

Sr. No	Perspective	CEO	Weight	Target
1		Finance 1: Market Capitalization / PE Multiple	20%	
2		Finance 2: EBITDA%	15%	
3		Finance 3: Working Capital / Net Cash Flows	15%	
4		Customer 1: Internal Customer Survey / Employee Survey	15%	
5		Process 1: Cash Conversion Cycle	15%	
6		Process 2: Initiatives Conducted to Increase Inter-departmental Communication	10%	
7		Learning & Growth 1: Implementation of the Balanced Scorecard	10%	

FIGURE 16.2 IPM (5–7 Measures)

Cascading Weights and Measures

When you select and assign weights to measures, you need to adhere to a logical process that can be applied throughout the organization.

Let me give you an example. We have a sales director whose performance measure is *company sales revenue* which is an aggregate of sales through different channels, such as key accounts, distributors, and online. It should be obvious that as we cascade to the next level down, the online sales manager's IPMs would include *online sales revenue.*

You can see how well this works by traveling back up the cascade. Every time you ascend to the next level up, you can see that the IPMs are aggregates of everything in the levels below.

The same concept works for weights assigned to each measure. For example, at the CEO level, financial measures might be weighted so they account for 40–55 percent of total performance (Figure 16.3). For the senior manager one level below the CEO, financial objectives might be weighted to account for 35–50 percent.

It's important to keep in mind that as you cascade down through an organization, the roles become more operational and less strategic. The measures should reflect this.

Typical weight for IPMs across functional areas within an organization

CEO		
Sr. No	Perspective	Weight
1	Financial	40-55%
2	Customer	15-20%
3	Process	20-25%
4	Learning & Growth	10-15%
5	Key Initiatives	10-15%

Senior Manager		
Sr. No	Perspective	Weight
1	Financial	35-50%
2	Customer	15-30%
3	Process	20-40%
4	Learning & Growth	10-15%
5	Key Initiatives	10-20%

FIGURE 16.3   Weighting Logic

Bands

I have never met a CEO who is fully satisfied with the competency and performance of his team. The reality is that it's not possible to fire everybody and replace them with better people. And it might not matter anyway. The executives' level of performance might have nothing to do with their capabilities as individuals, but rather come from weaknesses in the organization itself. What if the structure is wrong? Or the structure is right but the wrong employee is assigned to the wrong role? Or the employee is assigned to the right role but the performance measures and incentive program is off? Those are more likely to be the underlying problems.

I once executed a BSC for a U.S. Fortune 500 company that was one of the world's leading consumer electronics retailers, with over 2,500 stores. Data measuring sales by store was problematic, so we met with store managers and asked what was going on. The answer was simple, but sad. There were more than 52 different sales incentive programs running at any one time, and the store managers didn't have a clue as to how their performance was getting measured or what their sales incentive would be at the end of the week. For a job that is predominately dependent on variable compensation, that's completely unacceptable!

The purpose of having individual performance incentives is to motivate and drive individual performance, but this disorganized program was a huge demotivator. For the 2,500 store managers it meant low morale; for the company it meant missed targets. The convoluted incentive plan translated to underperforming stock, which impacted shareholders. Finally, it led to the firing of the CEO and management team, and Chapter 11 bankruptcy! If there is an example of how the wrong IPM framework can blow up a Fortune 500 company, there is no better example than this!

Therefore, the lessons you can apply to individual performance measures are: Keep it simple enough for employees to understand. Use clear logic that you can apply to all organizational levels. Make regular incentive distributions and pay in full so your credibility is high.

Finally, design a model that is flexible enough to be used consistently. For example, if a person achieves 80 percent of the target, pay 80 percent of the incentive bonus. If the person achieves 120 percent of the target, pay 120 percent of the incentive. Employees performing below 80 percent of target don't receive a bonus. You may want to cap the bonus amount at 120 percent, but you might want to make exceptions. Don't use too tight a band, like 90–110 percent. Your target setting will need to be very accurate, or people start gaming the system.

You may turn around and tell me it's too simple. My response is, "Well, go ahead and try the complex stuff with 52 different incentive plans, and enjoy the fireworks!"

IV

Challenges in Implementation

17

Selecting the Right Balanced Scorecard Coordinator

Not the Audit Team, Please!

Introduction

Over the years, one of the most common reasons I have seen Balanced Scorecard (BSC) strategy execution fail, is the selection of a weak coordinator. The selection of a BSC coordinator is not like selecting a project manager or a sponsor of a project. Projects have start and end dates, then people move on to the next thing. By contrast, running the BSC is running the performance-management and strategy execution process on an ongoing basis. The role is most closely related to the chief strategy officer (CSO) or chief financial officer (CFO).

It's probably a good idea to discuss the BSC coordinator's role in some detail, and then follow it up what makes a person ideally suited for the position.

The BSC Coordinator

The BSC coordinator's tasks change with the different phases of the strategic process.

Once a firm has decided to use the BSC to help execute strategy, it's time to figure out who will be the coordinator. In most cases where an external consultant is being used to facilitate the program, it's best to take the consultant's advice in understanding the coordinator's role and who would be best suited to the position. In situations where the program is run internally, it's still important to fully understand the role prior to the selection.

Role in the Design Phase

The BSC coordinator's primary nine responsibilities in the design phase are outlined in Figure 17.1.

1. *Updating the strategic planning process:* The BSC results in the modification of the strategic planning and budgeting process on a permanent basis. The BSC coordinator, therefore, needs to take the existing process framework and description, and update it to reflect the new process, timelines, and roles. This document needs to be shared with the executive committee or the relevant leadership team, so everybody is in the know.

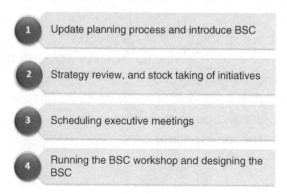

FIGURE 17.1 Role in the Design Phase

2. *Running an introductory BSC workshop:* This may become essential, especially if an external consultant is not being used. The BSC coordinator, with the CEO by their side, will conduct a two-hour presentation to the leadership team, introducing them to the BSC concept, its benefits, how the program will run, the associated timelines, and everybody's roles.

3. *Communication:* Once a decision is made to run the program, the BSC coordinator needs to work with the CEO or business head to develop a communication to go out to the entire enterprise. This memo will briefly introduce the BSC concept and explain why the program is being done, what it will look like, who is involved, and what the key milestones are. The aim is to request enterprise-wide support as the program is executed.

4. *Strategy review:* Since the BSC program is a strategy-execution and performance-management framework, taking stock of where the organization is in terms of its strategy formulation documentation is very important, as that is the basis of everything. This includes collating all the corporate, functional, and division-level strategic planning documents and taking stock of them. The documents need to be reviewed to get an overall sense of their quality and alignment with each other. In many organizations, one may find that the corporate-level documentation exists, but the next levels are missing or only partially complete. Also, these might reflect a weak alignment with corporate strategy. In some cases, all of the documents are weak, from a formulation perspective, and look more like budget documents. Taking stock of all these documents will give the BSC coordinator a clear sense of the current state of the strategic planning process within the organization. This could lead to a number of potential actions. In some cases, the documents might be so weak they need to be revised, and it is better to delay the start of the BSC program by six to eight weeks to give teams time to close the gaps and rework their

plans. In other cases, there could be gaps that are not worth delaying the program. In this situation, those gaps can be closed while the BSC process is underway. Finally, if everything is in reasonably good shape with some small gaps, the process can proceed as planned and the knowledge you gain can help in tightening up strategic planning the following year. While reviewing these documents, it's also important to review all budget documents and look for alignment—or misalignment—between key budget numbers and the strategic planning metrics. This is not uncommon.

5. *Taking stock of existing initiatives:* Collating the existing list of projects and their statuses, both at the corporate level and at the department level, is quite a task. The role involves looking at any project list and completing it. Often, projects aren't properly budgeted, so even the finance department's lists tend to be incomplete.

6. *Scheduling and participating in the one-on-one meetings:* For each BSC design, about 10–15 meetings with management need to be held. Scheduling those meetings is one of the roles that a BSC coordinator plays; the trickier part is participating in every meeting. As discussed earlier in the book, ideally speaking, at least for the first time a BSC is being designed and implemented, it is better to hire an external consultant due to their knowledge and lack of biases. If that happens, then the one-on-one meetings are done by only the consultant and the BSC coordinator is *not* in the room to allow for a free flowing conversation between the executive and consultant. Many BSC coordinators insist on being present, and very often we have to push back. If a consultant is not being used on a program, then the BSC coordinator plays that role. To succeed, the coordinator has to have the power and ability to engage senior leadership in a high-level conversation on strategy, and an unbiased discussion of the strengths and weaknesses of the organization and its leadership team— and keep it all confidential!

7. *Collating the findings:* Once the first six tasks are completed, the BSC coordinator needs to collate all that that they have heard and read and convert it into a 100+ page BSC workshop deck that discusses the internal assessment and external assessment, and develops the straw model Strategy Map.

8. *Running the BSC workshops:* The coordinator could run an actual BSC workshop in cases where an external consultant has not been hired. This is a full-day workshop where, by the end of the day, the moderator facilitates the management team as they agree on one version of the Strategy Map.

9. *Designing the BSC:* Using the final Strategy Map, the BSC coordinator (in the absence of an outside consultant) will work on identifying the measures, formulas, data sources, and the target-setting approach.

Role in the Implementation Phase

The BSC coordinator's role in the implementation phase pretty much stays the same whether a firm uses an external consultant or not. Implementing the BSC is the key role of a coordinator, not a consultant. The consultant can only guide. These are the tasks related to the implementation phase.

1. *Putting together the monthly reporting calendar:* Depending upon the time required to get organized for the first reporting period, the BSC coordinator will put together the calendar for the monthly BSC review. This is typically a two-hour meeting every month, with the executive committee and the CEO.

2. *Completing the monthly BSC report:* This requires updating the monthly BSC with the actuals, variance to targets, and the status of initiatives. Once the monthly BSC is completed, the coordinator should review it, make some strategic observations as to what is going right, what is going wrong, why, and what actions might be required to fix the problem.

3. *Facilitating the monthly review:* The BSC coordinator has to ensure that the meeting is facilitated well. This means guiding the discussion so it stays focused on addressing the issues and does not get too operational. The coordinator also keeps the conversation result oriented. Additional responsibilities include pacing the meeting so that it ends on time and clearly making note of follow-up actions required.

4. *Follow-up actions:* The coordinator ensures that all follow-up actions are completed, and progress is reported in the next session.

5. *Internal communication:* The coordinator creates internal communication themes resulting from the scorecard review. These are prepared for the rest of the organization to keep them aware of the overall strategic plan.

6. *Board reporting:* The coordinator could be asked to create a mini BSC for board reporting.

Picking the Ideal BSC Coordinator

As one can guess from reading all the above material, this is not a role for the fainthearted. It is a serious long-term role. Depending on how many BSCs are running within the organization, it could even be a full-time role. (See Figure 17.2.)

1. In my view this requires somebody who is the equivalent of the head of strategic planning, or no more than one level below that. This is not a human resources (HR) role unless the BSC framework is being used exclusively for individual performance management (IPM). This is also not a finance role because that runs the risk of treating the BSC as a management information system (MIS). Finally, this is not an internal audit role—unless you want the program to fail immediately. Nobody wants to deal with internal audit!

#	Desired attributes of the scorecard coordinator
1	Analytical skills are a must (financial background useful)
2	Strong leadership qualities
3	Good business understanding / overall awareness of general management issues
4	Excellent communication skills
5	Good interpersonal relationships
6	The scorecard coordinator generally is ▪ An aspiring candidate for business leadership ▪ Generally from finance/strategy department

FIGURE 17.2 Picking the Ideal Coordinator

2. The implication from all this is that the person must have solid seniority and be well respected within the organization. Good interpersonal and communications skills are required, but the coordinator must also be firm and not get pushed around easily. Because they will process a lot of information, they must also have sharp critical thinking skills and a strong understanding of the business's internal and external factors. They must follow up for any unfinished items intensely. Having some tenure within the organization is helpful, though not essential. The person must also see this role as a stepping-stone to something better ahead, like the head of strategic planning or leading a functional area or business unit.

Cascade Coordinators

This is an interesting issue. If a firm is running multiple score-cards, who should manage them all? Suppose a firm has a corporate BSC in addition to six cascaded BSCs. In this case, it's quite possible that a single individual working on a full-time basis might not be able to manage all seven scorecards. You have two options here:

1. Hire someone from a position just below the enterprise BSC coordinator, and have them all manage the enterprise and cascade BSCs as a team.
2. Hire cascade BSC coordinators that are embedded within the business unit. Adopt a matrix reporting structure, so these people report to both the business unit heads and the enterprise BSC coordinator.

I wish there were a simple answer as to which is the better structure. I have to say that it depends. If the business units are fairly strong and independent, there could be a good reason to pick the second option because the cascade coordinator will have a much higher sense of ownership. On the other hand, if the business unit is not that independent, or is underperforming, then I would recommend the first option because it will ensure that the BSC is being used for both communication and control.

No matter which type of BSC coordinator you are selecting, the bottom line on this is that you want one of your best brains to play this role.

18

Get Ready for the First Reporting

Sixty Days to Lift-Off!

Introduction

Just as strategy execution is often more important than the strategy itself, reporting the scorecard correctly and regularly is often more important than the design. Even if your design is 8/10, your Balanced Scorecard (BSC) execution needs to be 10/10. We are at the point now where the BSC has been designed and you are now getting ready for the first reporting, a process that is not as straightforward as it seems.

Timelines

Ideally, the delay from BSC completion to first reporting should be no more than 60 days. The reason is that if this key milestone is delayed, the initiative is lost; CEOs and executives get distracted and lose interest as some new business challenge or opportunity emerges. This can lead executives to demand changes in the BSC design, which basically means all the effort put in to this point was wasted. Another reason the first reporting should not be delayed is because changes to executive staffing can strike a serious blow to your strategy design. Not only do new leaders need to be trained in BSC practices and buy in to the process, but they will also want to make changes to the design to reflect their priorities rather than those of their predecessor. The worst scenario would be that the CEO leaves, the program has not started, and the new guy has no interest in the BSC program. I can almost hear what the new CEO would say, *"I need the first 90 days to understand the organization and the business, so let's put that on hold."* What he means is, *"I don't own that last CEO's strategy, so I am going to create my own"*.

To avoid falling into this trap, it is therefore important to get the first reporting going by the critical 60-day point, without getting bogged down by some tactical stuff. Let me explain.

Now that everyone is ready to report, it's time to collate the actual numbers. Let's imagine you are preparing to report November's scorecard. You need to be clear on where the data will come from, what formula you must use, and what the measure is. Let's say you have addressed some of this during the design phase. However remember you have not actually gone through a reporting cycle. You will find that once you try to report a measure, all of a sudden one data component of the formula is not available. In essence, making the measures unviable.

To take stock of the situation before you get stuck, I recommend taking the following steps, as illustrated in Figure 18.1:

1. Put the list of final measures on the table and write next to them: what is immediately available to measure in terms of available (AV) data; what can be measured but needs some modification (available with modification, or AVM), and those measures where the data is not available (NA). If you have 30 measures, you may have 18 AVs, 7 AVMs, and 5 NAs. This is a workable situation, as most of the measures are available, and so you can go into a reporting feeling prepared. However, if you report

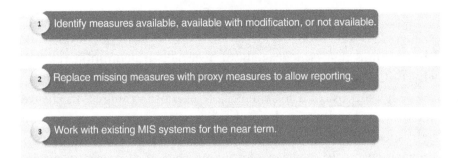

FIGURE 18.1   Collation of Actuals

with too many missing measures, then the entire BSC can be rendered useless and ineffective and almost dead on arrival.

2. If the situation were reversed and you had 18 NAs, you are in trouble. Finding suitable data for those NAs could take more than 90 days, and such a long delay will undermine the overall BSC. It therefore becomes necessary to consider using *proxy measures*. Proxy measures pretty much reflect what you would want from a regular measure. They can help you figure out if things are going right as far as the objective is concerned. For example, if you cannot do a customer satisfaction survey on a regular basis, the number of customer complaints is an appropriate proxy measure. If the related objective is to significantly enhance the customer experience, the proxy data can give you a clear idea of performance.

3. Finally, there could be issues about the sources of your data. Perhaps you originally selected the enterprise resource planning (ERP) system as your data source, only to discover the customer relationship management (CRM) system contains better numbers—if you can give them some massaging, that is. Do not get overly concerned about this. It's fine to change and use the CRM data, rather than taking a fixed position and waiting for a modification to the ERP system so it will give you the information you want. It might be in your best interest to avoid involving information technology (IT).

The Accuracy of a Measure

I have found that concerns about accuracy are common reasons why BSCs are delayed—and often fail. This is just plain silly.

The purpose of using the BSC to execute strategy is to ensure that we are heading in the right direction at approximately the right speed. That means that if business from repeat customers is approximately 70 percent, knowing that it's, more precisely, 70.299 percent doesn't make a difference. I know you think it's obvious, but you would be amazed how many firms and Scorecard coordinators chase the decimals. I call them the decimal chasers (DCs).

So to summarize on this point, don't get too statistical on a measure's accuracy. Just make sure it's reasonably accurate, and you will be fine.

You Missed the Start of the Year

This happens often. It would be ideal if everyone designed the BSC just before the start of the year, at the right point of the business planning process, and went into the year reporting the first scorecard. The truth is that 80 percent of the time this won't happen. The BSC program gets completed somewhere in the middle of the year for the first time, and that's okay. Sometimes CEOs will come under pressure from executives who say that with half the year gone, and an annual strategy already in place, it's best to wait until next year. *That's a trap!* The reality is that nobody likes to be measured frequently, and the executive is attempting to defer that situation.

I would get the BSC going within 60 days of the design completion, no matter what part of the year it is. How does it matter if the strategy is already complete for the year? The BSC is an execution tool. Simply take the strategy that has been agreed to for the year and start reporting progress on it using the BSC.

Another argument to expect is the complaint that the data is not in place because some of the new measures have not been regularly tracked. No problem. Revert to the *proxy measure* approach outlined above.

Then the next argument will be that we have not set targets for all the new measures. That's fine. Simply report the actuals without the targets. The benefit of doing that for at least half the year is that it will give you a sense of what target you should set for the next year, based on the reported actuals. Even better, you can set an estimated target using the best judgement of all the senior executives in the room. That's not difficult, especially considering compensation is not tied to hitting the BSC numbers. You are simply attempting to ensure the strategy is executed well.

One more argument is that people may be out of office for the holiday season. *We might as well wait.* This doesn't make sense at all. Your company is running. Your customers are buying. You can continue to measure performance.

The final example of a common argument for delaying the BSC is a change in staffing. Imagine that there is a new executive joining in 60 days. Some executives prefer to get started after she is on board. This argument is also faulty. The BSC is for the enterprise, not any individual, so it should be in place even if the leadership team is not fully staffed.

I have seen all these excuses and more. Don't let them trip you. As soon as you complete the design, get it going within 60 days. Lift off!

19

How Should the First Meeting Run?

And How Frequently?

Introduction

Finally, you reach the day to do the first strategy execution review using the Balanced Scorecard (BSC). As a CEO, you have ensured your presence, your BSC coordinator has ensured a good first reporting deck, you have blocked two hours on your calendar, and you have ensured that all members of your executive committee are present for this in person or over a video link. (No conference calls, please. They just don't work.)

The meeting should happen before the seventh day of the month (the window between the fifth and seventh is ideal) or you will not have time to benefit from your findings during the next month. The data should be available in your management information system (MIS) in time for you to prepare. If it is not, you need to fix that problem immediately, as it impacts the overall performance of an enterprise. An enterprise should be tracking its performance on key metrics on a daily basis, and the month-end

FIGURE 19.1   First Meeting

number is simply an aggregation of the daily data. *I would not give more than 48 hours to aggregate the month's data, meaning it should be ready by no later than the third day of the month.*

The first meeting, and every meeting that follows, will run a similar course, covering the five steps shown in Figure 19.1.

Deck Pre-distribution

The first BSC deck should be distributed about two or three days before the meeting. The meeting should not be the first time that everybody looks at the deck. By the time you sit down in the conference room, everybody should have read it, made their observations, thought about the challenges that are being reflected in the strategy, and how they can help fix it. Finally, each person should list things that are missing and need to be talked about.

Some executives may attempt to correct the measures or data at the last minute; this should be strongly discouraged. Necessary tweaks and adjustments should have been figured out before the deck was distributed. Now is not the time to do it.

Recently, I visited a client where one of the measures was *the number of sales calls per day* made by the company's internal sales force. The number was very low. The head of sales started harassing the BSC coordinator, claiming that the customer relationship management (CRM) system did not reflect the complete data because the sales team had not been regularly entering their calls into it. *Whose fault is that?* The BSC will report whatever data is in the system; there is no guarantee that the other numbers being suggested are any more accurate. To avoid this kind of embarrassment, the sales head needed to ensure that the sales force enter their data correctly and on time.

If you don't take a firm position, drama like that will never end, and you will be having the same conversation over and over again. I know BSC coordinators who don't sleep the night before reporting because tweaks and changes flow in right until meeting time.

Only genuine errors should be corrected in the days between the deck pre-distribution and the meeting, and hopefully it does not happen too often.

BSC Coordinator's Role

The BSC coordinator has ensured everybody has the deck and a copy of the BSC to be reported on the projector. He or she will start the meeting by quickly summarizing observations on the first couple of pages of the deck. Once that is done, it is not in the BSC coordinator's best interests to stand near the projection screen or speak as the BSC is being discussed. Coordinators are not responsible for reported performance, so they should leave the questions and defense to the people who own the objectives. *So many times, coordinators get carried away and try to take on a more visible role in directing the meeting.* Underperforming executives often attempt to pile on to the BSC coordinators by trying to make them explain the lack of performance on the objective. *Slow down.* The coordinator does not own any objectives. The person making all the noise should be the one explaining what's wrong. Other times, executives try to poke holes in the quality of the data, or if they get really desperate, say the measure is wrong. *Were you asleep when the BSC was being designed and not reading what was sent to you?*

If this kind of behavior persists, it's up to the CEO, not the BSC coordinator, to put an end to the nonsense and clarify that the executive is responsible for answering the questions.

After summarizing the top two pages, the coordinator should sit down and let the discussion begin. At that point the coordinator becomes a note taker on key points and ensures the meeting is not taking a direction that is too operational. Additionally he or she keeps time so the meeting can end on time and, if the coordinator is also a strategy head, takes part in the discussion to fulfill any operational role. As everyone becomes better practiced at reporting, these conflicts will come up less frequently.

The Discussion

What should first happen is everybody should take deep breath, switch off their cell phones, and spend the first 10 minutes looking at the Strategy Map and BSC that has been put up and make any additional observations or comments in their notes. *Absorb all that is there.* By the way, the budget documents should be on the table, showing actuals versus the variance in case anyone needs to refer to them.

The meeting should start with the *Financial Perspective*. Focus on the objectives that are in the red, where the target has been missed. The CEO should lead from here, turning to the owner of the first red. Let the executive lead the discussion of what is going on with that objective, provide a full context on why something is off track, and specify what their plans are to rapidly fix the problem. Let the person have their 10–15 minutes to talk. After that, it's time for everybody else to step in. *Remember that the role of everybody on the executive committee is to find solutions to the problems that face the enterprise.* Each of the executives who has an idea for how they can help and what the solution should be, should speak up. The CEO should be a keen listener, deferring comments until everybody has had a chance to speak. Then, the CEO can provide a concluding view, and summarize how they want the issue addressed, maybe even impressing upon the executive that time is running out and patience is limited, and that there is an expectation for the issue to be fixed prior to the next BSC meeting.

It is quite possible that the BSC coordinator has ensured that *drilled-down* data has been made available to make the discussion more substantial. Then that data must be looked at. Here is an *example*. The overall BSC is reporting total sales, but this is a function of sales by channel (direct, online, distributor). The additional numbers reveal that online sales are off, so the drilled-down information needs to focus on a channel discussion.

There is also a possibility that while the problem can be fully understood at the meeting and the solution is obvious, *the exact solution may need more data* and more operational executives in the room (*e.g. Why is the steam boiler failing regularly?*). This will then lead to a follow-up discussion either immediately after the meeting, or in the next day or so, so that the problem can be fixed. This does not need to be a face-to-face meeting, so it can take place like typical meetings at the firm (e.g., face-to-face, phone, or video).

There is also a possibility that the problem is resulting from *other people not doing their jobs*. For example, sales are down because not enough salespeople have been hired on time; human resources (HR) is responsible for that. In that case, the HR executive must join the discussion and explain what's going on, why there are delays, and provide a solution to the problem. In another case, it could be that the chief financial officer (CFO) has not released the funds to purchase raw material, resulting in production and sales shortages. The CFO might have made this decision to comply with a set of business rules that, based on this conversation, the company may decide to modify.

Once the discussion on the red line items in the Financial Perspective, is complete, its good to take a look at the green numbers. It's important to acknowledge positive performance and to understand what is working, or if the change is the result of a one-off situation. This will prepare people to see a red number next month, if that should be expected.

Once the Financial Perspective is done, move on to the customer perspective and follow the same process. The plan should be to take about 20–25 minutes per perspective in general, so you leave about 20 minutes to talk about initiatives and the last few minutes to close out the meeting.

The Discussion on Initiatives

The reason businesses run initiatives and projects and spend tons of money on them is to deliver the strategic objectives and enterprise performance. *Often that tends to be forgotten.*

Well, in the corporate BSC meeting, all we want to do is to look at the status of the top 10 projects, and to ensure they are on track to deliver our strategy. I recommend tracking these projects on an initiative template, an easy one-page document that provides an overview of key information (Figure 19.2).

Example Project Status Update

ID	Project	Priority	Function	Sponsor	Project Mgr.	Start Date	Next KMS	End Date	Issues/ Next Steps	Inv ($ Mn)	Benefits	Status
												●
												●
												●
												●
												TBP
												TBP
												TBP
												◐
												◐
												◐

TBP: To be planned

FIGURE 19.2   Initiative Template

What Makes a Project a Top-10 Project?

Even a simple question like this can have multiple answers, some of them wrong. In my view a top-10 project includes the following kinds of projects:

- Projects of significant financial value
- Projects that may not have a very high value, but have a material impact on the performance of an enterprise
- Projects that are very time sensitive

When reviewing projects, we follow the same approach that we used for objective review. First, look at all the projects that are in the red. Ideally, all strategic projects would have an executive committee sponsor who is present at the BSC reporting meeting. Let the person explain what's going on, why is it's in the red, and how and when will the problem be fixed. If necessary, let the *project manager* join this part of the meeting, lead the presentation, and exit after the presentation is done. Do the same with all the red items. Then quickly look over the greens, acknowledge the fact that they are performing well, and quickly confirm that they will continue to do so.

Tracking the Benefits I want to close out on this topic with a brief discussion on *benefits* that need to accrue from initiatives and how to track them. Very often firms implement projects because the investment is meant to bring some kind of benefit (e.g., reduced cost, more customers, shorter turnaround times, headcount reduction, new products, etc.). *However, very few companies track the benefits once the project is complete.* I am convinced that, just as the executive committee is tracking a strategic project's status, they must also track the benefits of projects completed, at least in the 24 months that follow, as that is how long it can take to realize results.

Track this on a table that includes the top 10 strategic projects completed in the past 24 months. Identify the resources invested, the expected key benefit, and what has really happened. Track each one for about 6–12 months until you are convinced that the benefits from the projects are sustainable or fully achieved. You can then take that project off the list and add a new one.

Meeting Closure

The last 5–10 minutes of the meeting should be a wrap-up of everything that was discussed. The CEO and BSC coordinator quickly summarize what actions and decisions were agreed to, who will do what, and what the next steps are. There is a quick discussion of next month's plan before the meeting comes to an end.

What about the Cascade Scorecard Meetings?

Cascade scorecard meetings follow the same format outlined above, with the respective cascade's management around the table. *Ideally, those meetings should immediately follow the enterprise BSC meeting*, as decisions made by the executive leadership can affect the cascade BSC.

Conclusion

You would be amazed that, while executives understand their operating roles, they are often no better than high-school students when it comes to effectively managing a meeting and ensuring an outcome. If you can't do that with your BSC monthly strategy execution review, your execution efforts will be seriously diluted!

20

What about Scorecard Automation?

Mobile and Dynamic Scorecards

Introduction

The topic of scorecard automation typically arises early in the Balanced Scorecard (BSC) process; often after the first BSC review meeting. Figure 20.1 provides an overview of how this automation flows.

The Excuse to Automate

As soon as the first or second review meeting is done, the BSC coordinator will suggest that the scorecard cannot be efficiently or accurately reported unless the process is automated. It's possible that an outside automation firm has gotten to them (*I know this*

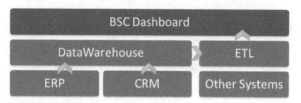

FIGURE 20.1   Scorecard Automation

*because my firm offers an automation solution—**Accelerator**)*, or simply because the coordinator believes life will be much easier with an automation solution in place. That is actually not true; I'll tell you why.

Most organizations do not have a robust management information system (MIS). In the early BSC reporting rounds, many of the measures may need to be manually calculated. At times, the data will need to be imported from multiple sources. Even automation solutions cannot fully get rid of this problem. *Automating your scorecards before automating most of your measures is not a good idea.*

There is another issue. It is quite possible that it may take two or three reporting cycles to finalize and freeze your data sources and your measures. What if you rush into automating your scorecard right after design, and find that, after three or four meetings, that the BSC design has changed? Then you have wasted a lot of resources automating a now-obsolete scorecard.

When to Automate?

The ideal time to automate is when your BSC has stabilized after two or three reports. If you are reporting cascaded scorecards, it is hard to simultaneously and manually manage all of them and, more importantly, their linkages. Organizations with a very strong MIS, might be able to use automation to dynamically review scorecards, even on a daily basis, not just at the end of the month. Most automation solutions are mobile, allowing the leadership team to view them on their desktops or tablets.

Components of BSC Automation

These are the three key components of a BSC automation framework.

1. *Your data sources:* These could be multiple data systems within your organization, including enterprise resource management (ERP), customer relationship management (CRM), financial systems, human resources (HR) systems, and so on. Each of these may have different relevant data for your BSC and business. For instance, ERP could have your manufacturing data, while CRM has your customer data.

2. *Your data warehouse (DW):* Your IT department could have bought a DW to allow for the current MIS to be aggregated within the enterprise without touching your core systems. These are also called *datamarts*.

3. *The BSC automation solution:* The BSC automation solution will have the following components:

    a. Extract-transform-load (ETL): An ETL platform that plays with the data it sources from the DW or from your systems, allowing you to manipulate it and combine it in useful ways. This is generally needed when dealing with large volumes of data.

    b. Business intelligence (BI) and dashboarding: A BI platform that also analyzes the data and displays it as a dashboard on your desktop or tablet. These could be proprietary BI solutions or those created using JAVA, Jasper, Qlikview, or other BI solutions.

    c. Hardware platform: The solution could be hosted either on a server in your firm, or on the cloud.

    d. Access rights: Different rights for different users. For example, the BSC coordinator should be able to update the Strategy Map and scorecard, and have full access to modify and update everything. A business unit head, on the other hand, may be able to see their unit scorecard, but not another division's.

The Automation Process: The Data Challenge

Typically it should take you six to eight weeks to automate your BSC, but it all depends on your data situation. Let me explain.

The vendor will need to identify the sources of data and how it will be accessed. *This is a huge issue.* In most organizations data sits in disparate systems. That means if the scorecard is to be automated, and the data is sitting in multiple systems, the solution will need to connect to multiple systems to pull the data—a *big* IT no-no! For banking applications where there are huge data security issues, it's almost impossible.

You may get lucky if your firm has a *data warehouse (DW).* Your DW sits on top of all your systems where most data aggregates, and is available. If your firm has that, you are in luck. Then most automation solutions will simply connect to the DW, and pull the data from there. But that is not enough.

The next question that comes up is: How much data do we need? This is a significant issue. For banks, where an average customer makes multiple transactions per day, the data for even a month could be many terabytes. The point I am making here is that the amount of data you need will determine how easy it is to implement a BSC automation system and the associated cost.

BSC automation also impacts the design architecture. If there is a large amount of data that needs to be processed, it cannot be simply fed to a BSC-type BI system (e.g. Jasper, SAS) to display. *It needs to be transformed.* That means you get stuck with another process and add-on software called an *ETL layer.* That means that once your BSC solution is connected to the database, you need another layer in between—an ETL layer—to make the information accessible. That also means that you need to hard-wire your data sources and formulas for the ETL to work, making the solution less agile.

Nowadays a lot of BSC automation companies are using *agile BI platforms*. These agile platforms allow you to rapidly change formulas and data outputs without significant recoding. For example, you may want to change what you display on the x-axis of a chart, or you may want to add a new division's revenues to a formula. Ideally, you would want to be able to do all of this without significant coding.

The point I wanted to make is that the biggest challenge in making BSC automation work is the data. Try to minimize the complexity of sourcing this data, and more importantly, don't let your IT staff give you a hard time about trying to automate the solution. This often becomes the issue. Sometimes we ask IT to give us the data in an Excel file, and even that becomes a challenge.

Benefits of BSC Automation

These should be the benefits of automating correctly:

- Ability to report multiple scorecards seamlessly.
- Better visuals, including charts that show trends.
- Ability to do dynamic drill-downs on the data to analyze cause and effect.
- Ability to have dynamic scorecards to see how things are changing, daily or by the hour, rather than waiting till the end of the month.
- Mobility. Having your scorecards with you on the go.
- Ability to modify/enhance the scorecards with minimal effort.

Of course one of the key benefits of automating the Scorecards is to bring stability and longevity to your BSC program. It will ease the reporting of the BSC, allowing the process to stay in place. Lastly, keep the investment light. I wouldn't spend more than $100,000 on a BSC automation project!

21

What Happens After a Meeting?

Making Sure the Traction Lasts the Whole Month

Introduction

Strategy execution using the Balanced Scorecard (BSC) is all about driving change. What's the point of having a very productive, solution-oriented meeting, if afterwards *nothing happens?* Everybody just goes back to doing their jobs the way they normally do, and then, a month later, shows up for the next BSC meeting for another two-hour discussion. That won't change anything.

This happens a lot. While all everyday operational actions contribute to the execution of strategy in some shape or form, you cannot achieve execution excellence if you fail to apply what the BSC review meetings reveal. Additionally, the alignment, focus, and prioritization that emerge from using the BSC framework, are critical for execution excellence. Execution excellence, when using the BSC, is as much about what you do between the meetings (Figure 21.1) as it is about what you do in the conference room. Figure 21.1 outlines the key activities post the BSC reporting.

FIGURE 21.1   After the Meeting

Circulation of Post-meeting Deck

The same day the meeting is over, it is critical for the BSC coordinator to create action points based on the meeting minutes, and circulate them immediately to all committee members. If the meeting has resulted in a need for the BSC deck to be updated, an updated copy of the deck should also be circulated. If the BSC is automated, then the next version of the BSC must reflect any changes or notes.

Follow-up Action

As I indicated earlier, execution excellence with the BSC is about driving change. This could result in a set of urgent follow-up meetings or actions to implement the solutions determined at the meeting or to more deeply investigate a problem.

1. The meeting could indicate that a number of committee members need to sit together and find a solution or detail an implementation step at their level without the involvement of other executives or the need for approval for additional resources. A simple, joint decision needs to be made.

2. Another result of the meeting could be that a solution requires the involvement of operational teams. This happens in cases when an operational solution can solve a strategic problem. Examples include: the failure rate on the factory floor requires an active discussion with the factory manager and the QA team; an underperforming call center at a bank requires a discussion between the retail banking and the call center head.

3. The meeting could indicate an urgent need to engage with a third-party. This can be necessary, for instance, to settle a matter with the tax department, renegotiate with a supplier, or offer a greater discount to a new customer.

The important point here is that whatever the actions are, they need to have a high sense of urgency, as they impact a strategic outcome, which in turn affects company performance. The BSC executive team expects that changes will deliver benefits within a relatively short period of time—even as soon as the next monthly meeting.

Complaining

The BSC process also results in a lot of complaining. Executives come out of a review and gossip, sometimes sarcastically, about the meeting or other executives. If you are worthy of being on an executive or management committee, speak up when you have a chance to do so or be silent afterwards. Whispering after the meeting is over doesn't accomplish anything, and I think it's for cowards. There are many ways of speaking up without alienating people. Here's an example: Rather than saying *"Your attempt to sell more through your distributors will fail,"* you could try, *"If you explore the online option, it may also help you generate additional sales."*

Ensure Cascade Alignment

If cascaded BSCs are also running at a departmental level, it may be necessary to exchange notes with them; there might be a need to realign the BSCs or share the output of the meetings with each other. Example: *The enterprise BSC has decided that there will be a company-wide hiring freeze for the next quarter. However, the cascaded*

BSC for the business unit had decided to increase sales by hiring more salespeople. This is a disconnect that needs to be addressed immediately.

Initiative Action

The review of the top 10 initiatives will likely result in a set of actions for some of those initiatives, but it could be more than that. There could be initiatives running at the enterprise level that are dependent on a top-10 initiative's output, or there could be initiatives at the next level that have similar dependencies. All of them need to be aligned, and getting there may result in a series of follow-up actions.

An Unfortunate Case Study: Blowing up a $5 Billion Company

Here's an example of an unfortunate situation where a client simply refused to take some follow-up action after the BSC meetings.

A few years ago, I had a major BSC mandate with one of the world's leading consumer electronics retailers, who had over $5 billion in revenue, and 5,000 small-format stores. The BSC exercise clearly showed that many of their stores carried dead stock worth a total of $250 million. Unless that stock was removed, resulting in a one-time write-down, the firm had no real way of returning to profitability. This action would have forced a rationalization of a number of outlets and the potential of creating space for what they called *small digital devices*. These products were driving traffic and sales for others in the industry, and this retailer had a huge opportunity to capitalize on this growing trend.

However, instead of putting a plan in place, the CEO told me that if he did the write-down, Wall Street would kill him, and he would lose his job. So nothing happened and no tough decisions were made. The losses continued and this retailer became one of the first companies on the planet to terminate a large number of employees via email. Then, they filed for bankruptcy. Every time I think about the situation, I feel really bad. This great company met a sad fate, and it all came down to the inability of four executives to make a few tough decisions that would have proved right in the end.

Think about this example if you are ever casual or feel lazy about a BSC meeting's follow-up decisions.

22

The Communication Challenge

It's Like Keys to the Executive Washroom

An Unfortunate Case Study: Paper on the Walls

I'm going to start this chapter with a case study to make a point. Many years ago, I went to see a client of mine in Lille, a small town in France. He was the CEO of one of the divisions of one of the largest French companies in the world. I walked into his conference room and noticed that every single wall was covered with many pages of PowerPoint slides. I asked him what was going on. He said that he was trying to communicate the strategy to his management team and factory leadership, so once a week, he made them come by the conference room and take a fresh look at all the slides to remind themselves of the firm's strategy. He thought this would help them stay focused. Wow! I thought people only looked at stuff on a wall at an art gallery!

I was speechless. This CEO is a really smart guy. He understands the importance of strategy and execution, and he had taken extreme actions to communicate this to his team. But it doesn't

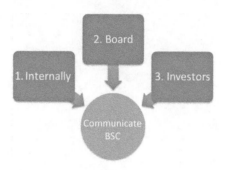

FIGURE 22.1   Communication Challenges addressed by the BSC

need to be that way! The Balanced Scorecard (BSC) can help you do the same thing through a formal process that is much more effective.

Figure 22.1 illustrates the communication challenge that the BSC helps organizations address. As you can see, the key stakeholders—internal audiences, the board, and investors—can understand corporate strategy and execution thanks to the BSC.

Start at the Design Stage

Once a Strategy Map is finalized and strategic themes are identified, you have a great opportunity to build a communications agenda across the enterprise. The BSC coordinator or the CEO can draft a series of messages to all employees indicating that the firm is seeking execution excellence in delivering their strategy and is using the BSC to do so. The memos should explain that as a part of the process a number of strategic themes and outcomes have emerged. These are important enough to core business that everyone should understand and focus on them. Clearly communicating these facts even before you start measuring performance with the BSC can have a noticeable impact. Employees are more likely to think about these points as they conduct their business day to day. Online banners and posters can help remind employees of the organization's strategy so they understand their roles in that larger context.

At the Reporting Stage

You will see *huge* benefits at the reporting stage. First, when you start reporting performance, you can update internal stakeholders on how the organization is actually performing on its key strategic themes. This new way of framing success can be a wake-up call for people.

I've seen CEOs, with BSC pins on their lapels, walk the corridors and stop to greet fellow staff members and ask how their scorecards are going. All of this works because, for most people, if it's important to the boss, it's important to them.

The BSC can also be used to explain your strategy to the marketplace, especially *equity analysts and investors*. They get to see all the financial statements, but very few understand them in a strategic framework designed to drive financial performance. You don't need to broadcast the full scorecard; revealing the strategic themes and the performance on the associated objectives is enough. One of my clients saw their stock price jump by 20 percent as a result of effectively using the BSC to communicate with investors.

Board Reporting

This is really a good one. Boards focus on financial performance and boring committee reports, but they never get to see strategy in action, or how execution results in financial outcomes. It's, therefore, a good idea to create a theme-based strategy map (the *lite* version) for the board to review. The board is never going to have the time or inclination to review a full scorecard, but they will look at a lite Strategy Map with six or seven key themes and some measures that are indexed to show performance. It makes the board more knowledgeable, which helps them to make more informed decisions. This is very important to CEOs, who often complain that a large chunk of their time is spent managing difficult board members, rather than focusing on the external markets and business environment.

Using It to Build a Training Agenda

This is another strong benefit of effectively communicating the BSC; you can use it to build a training agenda. One of the biggest challenges that human resources (HR) directors face is that they are often not sure as to what the exact training agenda should be. They can figure out what will be broadly useful—most of it is pretty standard—but by using the BSC, they can direct training dollars to things that improve strategy-driving competencies. Isn't that a better way to approach professional development?

Take for example, the strategic theme of *service excellence*. If service excellence is a theme that is being communicated as a BSC priority across the organization, wouldn't it make sense for an HR director to adopt it as one of the department's important training themes? Definitely. Simply communicating enterprise priorities using a BSC allows HR to organize a training calendar around the most practical and effective topics.

In conclusion, don't make the strategy and the BSC like the keys to the executive washroom. In order to execute the strategy, employees need to know what it is!

## 23

What Happens If Performance Does Not Improve?

Patience and Speed Go Together

Introduction

It's not uncommon that regular reporting of the Balanced Score-card (BSC) does not result in any short-term performance improvement, or any performance improvement at all. Many people believe this is a sign that the BSC program is not going well, and has become nothing more than a management information system (MIS) tool, at best. What happened? Figure 23.1 depicts the four major reasons people consider BSC reporting to be a failure. We will discuss each of these problems and the implications in further detail.

It's Not a Formula 1 Car

One of the clear benefits of a BSC is that it accelerates performance, but there are limits to that acceleration. Many executives

FIGURE 23.1   We Are Reporting But . . .

seek rapid improvement in a company's financial performance if they are using a BSC. There are many reasons this cannot happen. First, financial performance is an outcome to action taken on non-financial drivers—customers, process, people and technology—of a strategy. Even if rapid action is taken at that level, by the time the effect of that action has an impact and then percolates up towards a financial benefit, a quarter or two can go by. *A simple example can be seen in increasing sales by increasing the size of the sales force. Similarly, obtaining efficiency and cost benefits can come from implementing new technology.*

So no one should be surprised if it takes some time for meaningful impact to appear—especially as a financial benefit. Of course people should expect some indicators or progress to be made in the right direction. Some of the non-financial drivers should start gaining traction and their numbers should start to move.

It is also possible that certain benefits can accrue only when the *projects or initiatives* that support the related strategic objectives are completed. After all, that is why those initiatives were put into place. Let's look at an example. There is an initiative to improve the output of certain manufacturing plant by adding load-balancing equipment. Only after that project is completed, can the supported objective (i.e., increased manufacturing output) be met. Other objectives will flow from there, starting with fulfilling customer expectations in terms of products. Finally, the financial outcome of sales will be met. As you can see, performance relies on causal relationships.

What If There Is No Cause and Effect?

In some cases, projects will be completed and actions will be taken, but financial or other objectives are not achieved. One of the reasons for this is a problematic Strategy Map and BSC design. If the strategic objectives that you have selected have no bearing on financial performance—either directly or indirectly—or on any of the other key objectives, then you are not going to see an increase in performance.

A classic example focuses on quality improvement. While we all agree that high-quality products sell better, we also recognize that having high-quality products is not the only driver to generate sales. About 15 or 20 years ago, with new thinking from Deming and Taguchi, the quality movement was at its strongest, and rightfully so. Product quality, even from some of the world's largest corporations was not what it should have been. The automotive industry was a classic example. The Japanese method of manufacturing was a case study that provided lessons to all of us. In those days, even if the Japanese did a super job in terms of quality, we all know that was not the only reason their products outsold their American-made counterparts. Design, pricing, the quality of the dealer network, and their after-sales service all impacted consumer behavior. So, if your Strategy Map and BSC indicated that significant improvement in quality alone would help drive financial performance, and that was the only real objective you were focusing your energy on, you are likely to have been disappointed.

Nowadays, maybe due to an excessive focus on quality, or because of robotics, the quality standards between the larger firms has stabilized, which means the products have become more commoditized. One measure or one area of improvement is no longer enough to rely on for financial gain. Business models have become more complex, which is why an organized, methodical approach to strategy is so important.

Here's another example: Ten years ago, online sales accounted for about 25 percent of total sales in the consumer electronics industry. The remaining 75 percent was sold through stores. Back then, I had a consumer electronics client who was diligently measuring same-store performance and new-store sales and, based on that, assumed that everything looked good. In reality, their online sales model was not working, even though the market was rapidly moving in that direction. Unless they made investments to support online sales, and designated measures to track performance, the company would be in trouble.

It's always important to ensure that the strategic objectives in the lower perspectives of the BSC lead to benefits in the perspectives above them. Otherwise, your objectives, map, and BSC will not help you succeed. What's the point of taking medicine if you can't get better?

Too Many Reds

I had a client situation recently where the BSC has too many red measures. Out of the 40 measures the clients had selected to track, 30 were behind target. I took one look at the BSC, and needed a drink! Normally a BSC would have about 25–30 percent of the objectives off-track, not 75 percent. When so many objectives are in the red, not only is it totally demotivating, but it also makes me wonder if the business model is so badly broken that it can't be fixed.

When a Strategy Map and BSC have so many objectives behind target, the immediate fix is to refocus and reset the targets to make them more realistic and bring the number of reds under control. Try to get the reds down to a reasonable number, five to seven, and have the entire management team focus on fixing only those for now. Reset the targets to get them out of the red. Only once those five are fixed, will it be possible to move on to the others. As soon as you get those out of the red, turn to the next five and start working on those. This might mean that the execution of strategy is going to take two quarters more than what you had originally planned, but isn't it better to do that than to have 30 reds staring you down, leaving the committee too demoralized to take action.

There could also be another unfortunate reason why an organization has too many reds. *The business model might be truly and permanently broken, meaning it's time for drastic action.* This could mean a few things are going on. It's possible that the CEO initiated this problem, and now that he or she has fully broken the business, it is time to move on as there is nothing else to break. Another possibility is that the business model in its current framework is not viable any more. The company needs to be split in half, and part of it has to be sold, or even shut down.

Here is another example: A company has a division that supplies yarn to another captive division that makes textile products. After years of effort the yarn division is unable to meet quality standards at the price it needs. The yarn division relies on old equipment, and it doesn't have the technology to produce the cutting-edge yarns that new textiles need. As a result, all of the yarn division's performance is red, and it's pulling the textile division's performance down with it. If the textile division were to buy yarn from outside, its direct indicators would turn green. The simple but painful solution here is to exit/transact the yarn business to ensure the survival of another.

The CEO is Not Pushing the Agenda

Meeting after meeting, the same set of executives keep delivering reds, demonstrating their weak performance. They are not getting called out at the meeting or can cleverly talk themselves out of bad situations. The CEO is also uncomfortable calling them out in the meetings and worries about making them look bad in front of their colleagues. The solutions are obvious but the executives are simply not acting. Another meeting ends, and there's no further discussion on the subject until the next meeting a month later, when the same drama continues.

This is clearly not acceptable. If you are expecting execution excellence, this is not the way to get it. It's the CEO's responsibility to ensure that the executives act on the agenda; if they don't, there must be consequences, either in terms of financial compensation or future employment. I hate to say this, but if executives believe that no one ever got fired for not delivering on a scorecard, then maybe it's time to show them it *can* happen.

The Ownership of the Strategy Is Wrongly Placed

Strategic objectives have owners, who are supposed to ensure the delivery of the strategy. But what if we picked the wrong owners or, worse still, some of the team members are incompetent. Picking the wrong owners is not uncommon. I will give you a simple but classic example. If the objective is to reduce cost, is it the responsibility of the CFO or the leader of the business unit running excessive costs? You can't pick both, so who do you go with?

The answer is *it depends*. If the business head lacks appreciation of the importance and urgency of what needs to get done, or has a track record of failure, I would pick the CFO. If the business head understands the issue, but needs help on the numbers, I would pick the business head but also ensure the CFO supplies any needed support.

The point I am making here is that selecting ownership on strategy execution is not about simply taking the organizational chart and pointing to the people who seem to most logically fit the objectives. It takes thought, and an understanding of the current cultural context, the existing competencies within the system, and the objective's critical components. Before selecting executive owners for strategic objectives, these things must be clearly in place or the objective will not be on track.

The BSC Coordinator Has Taken Over the Agenda

This happens, too. The primary role of the BSC coordinator is to help facilitate strategic discussion and execution focus using the BSC. It's the role of the rest of the organization to deliver the strategy operationally. *Unfortunately the BSC coordinator has fallen in love with the BSC framework and has started to dominate the meetings.* Other symptoms of this are explaining everything that is going on, declaring what action should be taken, and not letting the executives speak up when they are really the responsible parties. This causes the management team to switch off. After all, ownership has shifted from them to the overly enthusiastic BSC coordinator.

The CEO must not just stand by in this situation.

The CEO Stops Attending the BSC Review

If the CEO has stopped showing up for the BSC review. I can guarantee you that your execution focus is on its last legs. Why will anybody take the approach seriously if the CEO clearly doesn't? In this situation, other executives can stay focused on doing their operational jobs, which, I am sure in some ways, will help in deliver strategy. That might be all they can do.

An absent CEO needs to be reminded that the BSC is not another executive MIS tool. Its purpose is to drive change by focusing on strategy to solve problems on a proactive basis. Like a budget review, a BSC review is not optional.

24

Running a Best-in-Class Project Management Office

You Can't Do It without a Command Center

Everything Is a Project

Projects are how we convert possibilities into realities; however, all projects are not the same. Some projects are small, while others are big. Some require detailed planning and complex processes; others need to be carried out dynamically and in a more flexible manner. Some are complicated, requiring multiple people and technology; others are more straightforward and easy to execute.

A project, which has a well-defined beginning and end, is designed to deliver a unique outcome in terms of product, service, or result. Based on this definition, most, if not all activities we encounter on a day-to-day basis fall under the category of a project, right from planning a party to getting a medical check-up. In business as well, we see more projects today than ever before. This can be a good thing. Approaching work like a project encourages people to be more disciplined and focused on delivering outcomes.

Managing several projects systematically and efficiently, and ensuring their successful outcomes, has often been a daunting task for many organizations. This is particularly true for larger companies or companies dealing with change. Program Management helps address this challenge. According to the PMBOK (Project Management Body of Knowledge), a program is a group of related projects and program management is the management of these projects in a coordinated and synchronized manner. Program management enables a firm to gain advantages and control, which may or may not be achievable by managing each of these projects in a stand-alone manner.[1] A program is directed toward achieving overall strategic and organizational objectives. It takes a wider and more comprehensive view of the organization. Projects are more focused on their individual outcomes, which together contribute to achieving the strategic objective.

The Evolving Landscape of Project and Program Management

The landscape related to project, program, and portfolio management has been constantly evolving. As firms spend increasingly large amounts of money on executing strategic projects and programs, we frequently see a new function related to program and project management, surfacing in firms all around us. A project management office (PMO) provides a formal setting for managing projects and programs. The PMO is in charge of the costs, risks, and benefits of the program as a whole. It ensures the realization of cost saving through synergies between projects and scale efficiencies. Additionally, it allows the firm, to implement consistent policies and procedures between projects.

---

[1] Project Management Institute. *PMBOK Guide*, 5th Edition, 2013, page 368.

Many have compared a well-established PMO to the central nervous system of an organization. Primarily it facilitates synchronization among related projects and ensures alignment between the strategy of the firm and individual projects. In essence, the PMO is a vehicle that manages the execution of the strategic goals and objectives laid out by the firm.

The Program Manager's Role

The role of the program manager differs significantly from that of an individual project manager. It is broader and more high-level than that of the project manager, who is typically responsible for his or her individual projects, the team and its outcomes. A program manager in that sense, forms a layer above the individual project managers and directs the coordination and linkages across the portfolio of projects.

The project manager's role entails both strategic and operational activities. He or she is responsible for envisioning and planning aligned projects, identifying and allocating resources, and identifying possible risks and assisting in their resolution. Operationally, the program manager should provide regular business and technical inputs, ensure frequent steering committee meetings, monitor progress, and provide updates to management on overall status. Additionally he or she should follow the discipline of maintaining updated project and program documentation and maintaining communication with all stakeholders.

An Effective PMO

Effective program management requires some key processes. There are two different ways to categorize these processes: by knowledge area and by process group. On the one hand, knowledge area processes are categorized by the purpose they serve.

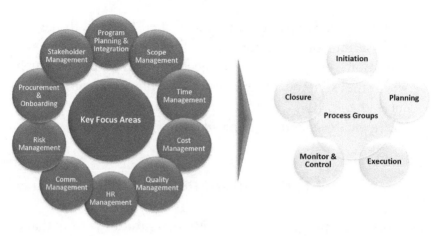

FIGURE 24.1   An Effective PMO

Process group processes, on the other hand, are categorized by the order in which they should be carried out. Figure 24.1 illustrates the knowledge areas and process groups used in both of these categories:

The tricky part, however, is that not all processes under a particular knowledge area fall under the same process group or vice versa. For example estimating activity resources and controlling the schedule, are in the same knowledge area, time management. However, resource estimation sits within the planning process group while schedule control is under monitoring and control. The subsequent pages provide examples of processes under these two broad methods of classification.

PMO Knowledge Areas

There are 10 key focus areas as outlined by PMBOK, also often called Project Management Knowledge Areas.[2] All PMO

---

[2] Project Management Institute. *PMBOK Guide*, 5th Edition, 2013, page 368

processes can be grouped under these 10 areas. Each area is characterised by the processes that fall under it; examples of typical processes in each area are as follows:

1. Program Planning and Integration:
   a. Creating and finalizing a program management plan
   b. Organizing integration forums
   c. Collating interdependencies across the program
2. Scope Management:
   a. Creating a scope and requirement management plan
   b. Collecting requirements through workshops and group discussions and collating them through precise documentation and a requirement traceability matrix
   c. Defining scope including creation of a Project Scope Statement
   d. Creating a Work Breakdown Structure
   e. Validating deliverables against scope
   f. Controlling scope through variance analysis
3. Time Management:
   a. Creating a schedule management plan
   b. Defining key activities and key milestones
   c. Sequencing activities by calculating leads and lags, using a precedence diagramming method, and creating a project schedule network diagram
   d. Estimating activity resources
   e. Estimating activity durations
   f. Developing a schedule using the critical path technique
   g. Controlling the schedule including resource optimization, schedule changes, and schedule forecasts
4. Cost Management:
   a. Creating a cost management plan
   b. Estimating costs

   c. Determining budgets

   d. Controlling costs and creating forecasts

5. Quality Management:

   a. Creating a quality management plan

   b. Creating quality checklists

   c. Performing quality assurance through audits

   d. Controlling quality including review of quality checklists and change requests and inspecting deliverables

6. Human Resources (HR) Management:

   a. Creating a human resources plan

   b. Assembling project teams and maintaining staff assignments and calendars

   c. Developing project teams and assessing performance

   d. Managing project teams including resource conflict management

7. Communication Management:

   a. Creating a communication management plan

   b. Managing communications including the use of formal and informal models

   c. Controlling communication through maintenance of communication logs, when necessary

8. Risk Management:

   a. Creating a risk management plan

   b. Identifying risks and creating a risk register

   c. Performing a qualitative risk analysis including conducting an impact assessment, categorizing risks, and assessing risk urgency

   d. Performing a quantitative risk analysis including risk modeling

   e. Planning risk response including formulating negative risk mitigations and positive risk strategies

   f. Controlling risks and facilitating risk audits

9. Procurement and On-boarding:
   a. Creating procurement plans and statement of work (SOW)
   b. Conducting procurements including proposal evaluation, negotiations, and vendor selection
   c. Controlling procurements including conducting procurement performance review, and reporting and facilitating inspections and audits
   d. Closing procurements
10. Stakeholder Management:
   a. Identifying stakeholders and creating a register
   b. Conducting discussions with different teams and creating a stakeholder management plan
   c. Managing stakeholder engagement including regular communication and creation of an issue log
   d. Controlling stakeholder engagement

PMO Process Groups

Processes can be grouped under five process groups, which are analogous to a project lifecycle. They progress from initiating to planning, executing, monitoring, controlling, and, finally, closing activities. Each group has a distinct set of process. Examples are listed here under each of the five categories:

1. Initiating Processes:
   a. Gathering data to initiate a project
   b. Defining key elements of the project and creating a project charter
   c. Identifying stakeholders
   d. Authorizing a project

2. Planning Processes:
   a. Outlining how a project will be managed and the overall project scope
   b. Creating a master project plan, schedule and charter
3. Execution Processes:
   a. Enabling coordination and collaboration among process groups
   b. Identifying risks and issues and propose mitigations
   c. Updating management on progress
4. Monitoring and Control Processes:
   a. Monitoring the project schedule
   b. Highlighting deviations from the schedule and proposing corrective actions
5. Closing Processes:
   a. Formally closing each phase and the overall project
   b. Obtaining sign-off from stakeholders after completion

The set of activities in each process group and the length it takes to execute them varies from project to project. A general rule of thumb is that execution processes require the most number of resources and take the longest, followed by planning processes.

PMO Maturity Levels

Obviously, not all firms have uniformly developed program management capabilities. The maturity of the firm's internal capabilities and processes help determine how equipped it is to effectively handle the planning, execution, and management of multiple simultaneous projects. An objective assessment of the firm's internal capabilities reveals how mature these are. All firms

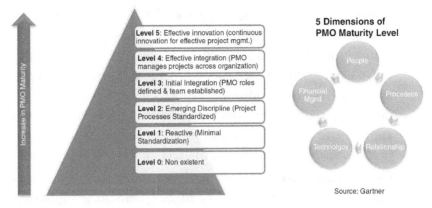

FIGURE 24.2   PMO Maturity

typically fall into one of the six progressive PMO maturity levels defined by Gartner. Figure 24.2 depicts these six levels.[3]

Each of these levels is characterized by the maturity of the five dimensions relevant to program management: people, processes, financial management, technology, and relationships. The maturity of a firm's PMO is directly correlated to the maturity of these dimensions. The firm's goal should be to continually develop and build an increasingly sophisticated approach to program management, that is, it should aim to move forward through the levels to allow for incremental benefits while ensuring there are no conflicts with organizational culture and no disapproval by stakeholders.

PMO Types and Approaches

Just as each firm has a different level of PMO implementation maturity, the type of PMO that would be most suitable differs from organization to organization, depending on industry, people, culture, purpose, and multiple other factors. Broadly, PMOs are often classified into the following categories:

---

[3] Gartner. "Toolkit Best Practices: Program and Portfolio Management Maturity Level," July 13, 2007. (http://www.strategies-for-managing-change.com/support-files/gartnerprogramportfoliomaturitymodel.pdf)

- **Supportive PMO:** These types of PMOs provide case-by-case support with regards to expertise, best practices, templates, training, and guidance. They are typically adopted by firms where projects are carried out with a lower degree of enterprise control; additional regulations and constraints are often not required in these situations. Many consider this approach to be a repository of project management information accessible to all project managers.
- **Controlling PMO:** Across activities, processes, and procedures, the level of control is higher than in a supportive PMO. This requires the adoption of specific methods and templates, and adherence to governance across individual projects. Projects also have to periodically pass reviews by the PMO. A critical factor for the success with this type of PMO is management support and sponsorship.
- **Directive PMO:** The directive PMO has more oversight than other types of PMOs. Here, project managers from the PMO are assigned to projects. Each manager reports directly to the PMO, so there is a high degree of standardization in processes across projects. This type of PMO is typically seen in larger organizations.

In addition to classifying PMOs based on their involvement and approach, another method to categorize them is from an organizational point of view. A PMO can be either enterprise wide, overseeing projects across the organization, or specific to a particular unit or department. In some cases, a special-purpose PMO is set up to achieve a particular objective.

Critical Success Factors to Set Up an Effective PMO

We now understand what a PMO is, as well as its benefits, processes, and the activities it covers. We have also learned how the definition of an effective PMO differs across organizations. It is worthwhile to summarize the critical factors to bear in mind while setting up a PMO. In my opinion the following six are essential to institutionalize a best-in-class PMO:

1. The PMO should clearly comprehend the organizational objectives and strategies. The PMO itself also should have well-defined, achievable objectives aligned to the enterprise strategies. Only then will it be able to translate this to achieve the expected outcomes on individual projects.
2. Regular and effective communication regarding organizational change is required to ensure acceptance and to avoid potential resistance.
3. Well-defined and documented processes, policies, and templates are required to ensure standardization across activities.
4. Strong governance, accountability of participants, and presence of relevant metrics to track performance is critical to ensure that the PMO methodology is adhered to.
5. High visibility and management backing is key to ensure adoption across the organization.
6. The PMO should have the appropriate level of authority to make decisions on projects and initiative-required actions. Some of this authority should cascade down to individual project managers. This would ensure that key project tasks and can proceed unhindered.

Linking the PMO to Strategy through the Balanced Scorecard

A critical aspect of implementing a successful PMO is to ensure its linkage to the organization's overall strategic objectives. One way to achieve this is to integrate the concept of the Balanced

Scorecard (BSC) in the project selection criteria. The following steps outline how this can be done:

1. Take stock of all existing strategic initiatives and projects.
2. Map these projects to objectives identified using the BSC framework across the Financial, Customer, Process, and Learning and Growth (L&G) perspectives.
3. Eliminate or discontinue projects that do not align with the firm's strategic objectives.
4. Identify additional initiatives required to achieve these objectives.
5. Prioritize based on strategic importance and a thorough cost-benefit analysis.

Following these steps would ensure that the PMO effectively manages the execution of the firm's strategy.

Let me explain what I mean with an example. My firm recently engaged with a leading commercial bank in the Middle East, with over 350,000 customers, 40 branches, and 180 ATMs. The bank had acquired the UAE retail and SME banking business of leading UK-based multinational bank. As a result of this acquisition, 235,000 customers were added to its portfolio. The selling bank retained the corporate banking portfolio, and had 90 days to separate the retail portfolio and have the ownership transferred. Apart from the complexities involved in a merger and acquisition (M&A) integration, this engagement had an additional element of separation, which had to be managed smoothly without any service interruptions for customers.

We approached this engagement by leveraging our deep heritage in the BSC. Building on the BSC ideology, a framework was designed to program manage integration across finance, customer, process, organization, and information technology (IT). The aim of doing this was to drive the following:

- A developed integration framework across work streams: integration PMO; integration planning and coordination across finance, customer, product, credit, process, channels, infrastructure, organization (HR), and IT.

- Identified key integration objectives for each module using scorecard framework and work-stream plans covering activities, tasks, timelines, milestones, teams, and deliverables.
- Overall migration planned in four waves: Legal Day 1 (separation of retail portfolio), channel integration, liability integration, and card integration.
- More than 55 applications affected in the integration: replaced, upgraded, or consolidated, including migration of data from an outsourced card platform managed by a Greece-based vendor to a UAE-based card-processing vendor.
- Specialist resources assigned to internal teams with periodic updates to project working and steering committee governance forums.
- Designed a customer communication plan across five products, and oversaw the execution including the target audience, content, channel, and frequency.
- Assessed overall synergies across all work streams and identified potential opportunities for revenue enhancement and cost savings.
- Developed an end-state operating model for effective utilization of the acquired shared service unit and centralization of all key back-office processes.

This structured approach of program managing the integration using the BSC framework ensured significant benefits for our client, some of which are as follows:

- Successful and timely integration.
- The bank's credit card portfolio was among the top three in the UAE following the integration. This type of growth could have taken the bank four times as long to achieve through organic growth.

- A 30 percent increase in the number of high-wealth customers, driving the bank to a leadership position in this demographic.
- The smooth integration of over 5,000 employees, a 20 percent increase in headcount.
- A seamless migration experience for customers across two branches, 51 ATM/CDMs, Internet and mobile banking channels, and a customer service call center.

This was a clear case of how the strategic objective of successful integration was executed through effectual program management!

## 25

Oops. The Strategy Has Changed

What Happens Now?

Introduction

Nothing lasts forever, not even strategy. Strategy could change during the course of a financial year, and it must change at the end of the financial year to prepare for what lies ahead. Either way, a change in strategy requires a change in approach to strategy execution, and the potential projects that are supporting them. So what do we do?

Midyear Strategy Change

There are many reasons strategy can change midyear.

- **There is a significant change in market conditions.** Regulations have changed. Competitors have decided to merge. A disruptive technology has shifted customer needs. A new distribution or service channel has been created. The financial markets have collapsed. There has been a national tragedy or an act of war. All of these events impact the markets and your business.

- **There is a significant internal change.** A division has been closed. A plant has been shut down. A product has been discontinued or started. A new channel has kicked in. There has been a factory strike. There is a major financial loss. These are especially difficult challenges to overcome because they can impact your competitive edge.
- **Leadership change.** There's a new CEO, who has a unique view of the future. It may be last on this list, but it happens often.

I am less forgiving about strategy changes that happen midyear due to internal factors. Internal factors are always within our control more than external factors, so when they force us to change, we are partially responsible. Often we should have done more to predict them, and integrate them into our strategy from the start.

If you have no choice but to make a change, see if you can time it to coincide at the end of a quarter. That will help, at least from the standpoint of aligning financial reporting of the BSC. In any case, this is how I would change the BSC midyear:

1. Look at the strategic objectives, and figure out which ones are seriously impacted by the midyear change. I am not comfortable tinkering with the whole scorecard or strategy map. Change only what you must and try to minimize the number of objectives you touch. If changes impact a connected objective, delay the change if at all possible.
2. Look at the measures affected by the change of objective, and make the necessary changes. Again minimize how much you do. If a measure needs to be eliminated, do so. Avoid playing with all or many of the measures at all costs.

3. Look at the targets and make appropriate changes based on the above changes.

4. Shut down any projects that are no longer relevant or add a new one, if needed.

You get my general drift. Make only those changes that are necessary so that you don't disrupt the ongoing BSC process for the year. Remember that if you are running cascades, too many changes could even affect them, forcing a major reworking that causes turmoil.

If you must change the BSC's direction because a new CEO is coming aboard midstream, I recommend people stand by their work and support the existing strategic processes. You may not be able to stop a new CEO from making major changes, but it's worth a shot.

The BSC does not reflect the vision and focus of a single individual, but the organization as a whole. If this were not the case, the process to develop a Strategy Map and Scorecard would be much simpler. There would be no workshops, no one-on-one meetings, no discussions with the management team; one meeting with the CEO would be adequate, and the monthly strategy review would have only the CEO dominating. There'd be no room for a BSC coordinator or management objective owners. It would be a one-man show!

My recommendation to new CEOs is to take a careful look at the Strategy Map and BSC to understand the collective views of the organization on its strategy and execution focus. Ask all the questions you want. If you feel you are forced to make changes, call for a meeting with the leadership team, and explain your point of view. Get as many of them to agree with you as possible. Moderate your view if they give you a new perspective. Then, finally make the changes that you feel you have no choice but to make, but minimize them and their effects. You will have soon a chance to do a more thorough review when the new fiscal year starts. In the meantime, working with the current strategy can help you understand how the organization works and what your new colleagues prioritize.

Annual Strategy Review

This is a process that businesses must go through at the end of the year. Using the BSC to update strategy and execution framework can help complete the process rapidly and seamlessly.

1. Ninety days before the start of the next fiscal year, is a good time to review how the year is going and how it is likely to end from an operational, financial, and, more importantly, from a strategic perspective. Completing this analysis may require some external market assessment to be done.

2. Capture all of this analysis, and head for a one-day off-site meeting with your leadership team. The first three hours should focus on internal and external reviews. Identify key changes in the market or your business, and how they may affect your existing Strategy Map and BSC.

3. Put up your existing Strategy Map and determine which strategic objectives are affected and need to be changed for the coming year, and which will not change. In my experience, unless there has been a major event, only 20 percent of the objectives will go through any change. Here's an example: If your existing strategy map has an objective saying, *"Enhance your customer experience"* it's quite likely that this objective remains the same for the next year. Then, there may be some objectives where the intensity has changed, so make the appropriate change. For example, you may not need to *significantly* reduce cost; simply reducing costs might be sufficient.

4. Then, look at the BSC, and look at the ownership, and see if any changes need to be made to the objective owners. Agree to those.

5. Then move to the measures and decide on any measures that need to be added or dropped.

6. Move on to the targets. This is the most interesting part of the process. Based on the revised strategy for the year, set your targets, using the approach discussed earlier. The interesting thing is that some of the previous year's *aggressive* objectives may have become *realistic*. You might also add new ones that are *aggressive*.

7. Lastly, look at the list of initiatives. Any of the initiatives that have been completed are no longer required, and new ones may need to be added for the year.

The benefit of using this framework to execute strategy, is that updating the BSC for the next year is an easy process to complete, and it actually helps simplify the strategic planning process. You will appreciate this benefit even more if you attempt to update strategies the old-fashioned way once you've become accustomed to the BSC method.

We are not quite done yet. Finally, the budgets need to be created, keeping the updated strategy and BSC in mind. The BSC outlined targets for the top 30 strategic measures and targets. The budget must reflect not only those, but also the operational numbers behind them. These targets, therefore, need to be inserted into the budget and a full budget needs to be created. If doing this creates a situation that indicates to us that some of the target numbers we set in the BSC are unrealistic or have unintended consequences, the BSC targets would need to be changed. Hopefully an organization needs to iterate only a couple of times before it's done.

Updating strategy should not be as hard as executing it, and the BSC ensures this is the case.

V

Conclusion

26

Conclusion

We are about to come to the end of our journey. My first book could be read in two hours, the length of a short commercial flight. I like to read books when I fly and I know other businesspeople also like something to quickly read and absorb before getting back to the real world. Despite my best intentions, this one has been a bit longer, as strategy execution is complex and I wanted to make sure I left something behind that you could use and reuse in days to come.

What I am going to try to do in this last chapter is to summarize all the key points I have made through out the book. But I will also be somewhat philosophical. Hopefully, this review will help synthesize your thoughts as you look ahead. This chapter will also help those readers who like to take a peek at the end of a book before they read the rest of it. It will give those curious people a nice overview of what they can expect to find inside.

Make Your Strategy Positive

Strategy is about execution. If you can't execute the strategy, it's not worth having. As I indicated earlier, never fight a battle that

175

can't be won. Every time you think about strategy and how aspirational and brave you want to be about it, make sure you have the people, fiscal, and technology resources to implement it and you know how to get there; you have your own Google Map—in this case your Strategy Map—guiding you.

Don't let anybody call a document that takes a 30,000-foot view a *strategy document*. Such blue-sky thinking is impossible to implement and will only lead to discouragement. Flying smoothly at 30,000 feet and enjoying the view alone does not make you a pilot. You need to be able to make a successful landing. In strategic execution, this means you need to know how to do that and have the execution framework to lead you there.

Don't let your strategy be more of the same—*incremental*, as we say sometimes. That has become somewhat of a habit in the more mature markets of the West. Gross domestic product (GDP) growth rates of less than four percent have become an excuse for many business leaders to play it safe and leave creative ideas on the table. In fact, the only "strategy" that they can really think about is reducing costs, and that's hardly rocket science. It's a numbers game, sometimes about headcount, where people lose their jobs., How about developing a strategy that protects people's jobs, and goes so far as to create more? If you can do that without fudging the numbers, you've found a real path to growth. Strategy is meant to support all the positive things business has to offer, such as new product development, innovation, double-digit growth rates, new plants, new partnerships, new technology, new markets, and a great belief in the future.

Unfortunately, it seems that the only markets where we see some of this spirit and optimism nowadays are in emerging markets like India and China. Every time I visit an emerging market with Western executives, I hear the same comment: "*I am impressed with all the positive energy.*" Well, how about taking back some of it back with you to infuse into your core markets?

Don't think in series. Unfortunately, business schools have taught us to think in a highly structured manner, asking all the right questions and crossing all the T's. Complete one task before you move to the next, they say. In such a rigid process, we lose sight of opportunities—we even overlook the fact that if we did everything in series, we may not achieve everything in our lifetime. *Parallel processing is key to a successful strategy*, along with organic and inorganic growth, product addition and deletion, adding new markets and closing some old ones, limiting old channels and adding new ones, valuing existing competencies and embracing new ones. In short, it's about yin and yang.

Execution Is about Focus

Let's have a positive strategy and focus on key parts of it in order to execute it. That's where the Balanced Scorecard (BSC) comes in, to ensure execution excellence in driving strategy. Identifying the top 20–25 objectives is the first step to honing your focus.

Do you know how hard that is to do? For many CEOs, everything is important. They can't seem to prioritize and stick with their choices. Starting at the top, with the ultimate financial objective: maximization of revenue, maximization of profits, and maximization of market share? You can't have it all. Realizing that, many CEOs decide that the real strategic challenge isn't execution at all—it's selecting the objectives! Luckily, the BSC gets you there, in a framework as logical as possible.

To meet financial objectives, meet customer objectives, and excel at key processes, ensure you have the best process enablers in terms of people and technology.

Make sure all your objectives are linked, so you aren't doing anything that doesn't ultimately help meet your financial targets. It really does not get any more logical than this, and it also doesn't get any simpler. This has worked for companies based in the world's largest cities, and also in countries you would never travel to. We are definitely onto something, which is why the BSC has remained one of the world's leading strategy execution tools all these years.

Focus and Measurement

That's what we tell our kids, right? Doing well in our exams means staying focused when we study, and measuring our performance with good grades. How soon we forget that the same rules govern our daily lives as executives. This approach can't apply only to financial measurement. That's like saying it's good enough to succeed in math and fail in all your other subjects. As executives we can't just deliver the financial numbers because they rely on the customers, the processes, the people, and the technology we work with every day.

We can measure our way to success, provided we have the right kind of measures, a combination of lead and lag, the right units, the right frequency, and, most importantly, the right set of *targets*.

Ownership

Own the strategy, and execute it with your team as if you owned the firm you work for. Make every decision as if it affects your personal and financial well-being and legacy. Be a team player, and don't complain if you work for a family-owned business—family members have capital at risk.

Stay on Track

Once you start the journey, stay with it. Report every month. Be solution oriented. What would life be if there were no problems? There will always be a problem that needs to be fixed. The whole idea is not about finding a road with zero bumps, but to predict where the bumps are and weave around them.

Don't change your strategy every day; if you do, you will forget where you started and you could wind up traveling in circles—or worse, run over the side of a cliff called *bankruptcy*. The landscape is littered with too many examples for you to believe that it couldn't happen to you.

Youth Matters

Are you surprised that all the new and successful firms are started by younger people? You rarely find an older guy starting a firm. Is it that because the younger lot were not seen to be valuable to traditional enterprises that are familiar to older people like us? How come older people usually have to buy young, small, innovative companies instead of incubating their own?

The reality is that we continue to underestimate the value young people can bring to an enterprise, and its ability to be successful. We marvel at their multi-tasking capabilities, but don't know how to leverage them. It's like we are creating two eco-systems. Places like Silicon Valley, whose value is worth more than 12 countries put together, and everybody else. Youth matters, and the more you make it part of your ecosystem, the more likely you are to achieve success.

Gray Hair Matters

Like youth, gray hair still matters. Experience counts. Battle wounds can remind us to look ahead and learn from the past. While the world has ignored the young, it has also discarded the old before they have run out of energy and ideas. The "strategy" called cost-cutting tends to ensure that this has happened.

Finally, executing strategy should be fun and give you a sense of achievement, a chance to excel.

Make your strategy work, and enjoy the ride!

Appendix A: Industry and Function Specific Strategy Maps and Scorecards

Pharma Research and Development (R&D)

Information Technology (IT)

Human Resources (HR)

Retail Strategy Map

Financial

- **F1** Drive profitable growth and shareholder value
- **F2** Grow same-store sales
- **F3** Grow country, website, and new retail formats
- **F4** Execute wireless, and the right assortment
- **F5** Improve inventory turns, optimize RE, and manage wireless risk
- **F6** Improve store labor effectiveness

Customer

- **C1** ABC understands my needs, and meets my expectations
- **C2** ABC is my first preference for technology products and services
- **C3** I find the shopping experience at ABC convenient and easy
- **C4** ABC's staff are readily available, knowledgeable, and helpful

Internal Processes

- **IP1** Continuously map customer and market, and act rapidly
- **IP2** Innovate and execute new channel additions successfully
- **IP3** Improve marketing effectiveness
- **IP4** Improve integrated assortment planning process
- **IP5** Transform store operations
- **IP6** Significantly improve decision-making processes

Innovation

Operational Excellence

Learning & Growth

- **L1** Develop a performance- and customer-centric culture
- **L2** Identify, develop, and reward field staff
- **L3** Improve competency in key positions
- **L4** Transform IT to enable business
- **L5** Improve employee engagement

Retail Scorecard

	Obj. #	Objective		Measure	Unit	Freq	Objective Owner	MTD Actual	MTD Target	YTD Actual	YTD Target
FINANCIAL	F1	Drive profitable growth and shareholder value	1	Revenue	$ Bn	M	CEO/CFO				
			2	EBIT	$ Mn	M	CEO/CFO				
			3	Shareholder value (EPS)	$	Q	CEO/CFO				
	F2	Grow same-store sales	1	Same store sales growth	%	M	Head of Sales				
	F3	Grow country, website, and new retail formats	1	Country rollout	KMS	Y	Head of Sales				
			2	Website revenue	$ Mn	M	Head of Sales				
			3	New retail format revenues	$ Mn	Q	Head of Sales				
	F4	Execute wireless and the right assortment	1	Wireless revenue	$ Bn	M	Head of Sales				
			2	Revenue growth (Key categories)	%	M	Head of Sales				
	F5	Improve inventory turns, optimize RE and manage wireless risk	1	Inventory turns	Nos	M	COO				
			2	New locations performance	%	Q	COO				
			3	Revenue/ rental cost ratio	Ratio	Q	COO				
	F6	Improve store labor effectiveness	1	Employees meeting productivity norm	%	Q	COO				
			2	Gross margin return on labor	%	Q	COO				
CUSTOMER	C1	ABC understands my needs, and meets my expectations	1	Customer survey	Index	Q	Head of Sales				
	C2	ABC is my first preference for technology products and services	1	Customer survey	Index	Q	Head of Sales				
	C3	I find the shopping experience at ABC convenient and easy	1	Customer survey	Index	Q	Head of Sales				
	C4	ABC's staff are readily available, knowledgeable and helpful	1	Mystery shopping	Score	M	Head of Sales				

Obj. #	Objective		Measure	Unit	Freq	Objective Owner	MTD		YTD	
							Actual	Target	Actual	Target
IP1	Continuously map customer and markets and act rapidly	1	Research plan	KMS	Q	Head of Strategy				
		2	Successful products launched	%	Q	Head of Strategy				
IP2	Innovate and execute new channel additions successfully	1	New store formats set up	Nos	Y	COO				
IP3	Improve marketing effectiveness	1	Promotions effectiveness	%	Q	Head of Marketing				
		2	Store traffic/advt. spend $	Nos	Q	Head of Marketing				
IP4	Improve integrated assortment planning process	1	Sub2 meeting revenue targets	%	Q	COO				
		2	Sub2 meeting inventory turn targets	%	M	COO				
		3	Gross margin return on space	%	M	COO				
		4	Gross margin return on inventory	%	M	COO				
IP5	Transform store operations	1	Conversion rate	Ratio	Q	Head of Retail				
		2	Procedure audit score	Score	Q	Head of Retail				
IP6	Significantly improve decision-making processes	1	TAT's	%	Y	COO				
		2	Charter of authority	KMS	Y	COO				
L1	Develop a performance-and customer-centric culture	1	Employees with BSC aligned IPMs	KMS	Y	Head of HR				
		2	% Pay at risk-linked to ABC goals (EPS/profits)	%	Y	Head of HR				
L2	Identify, develop, and reward field staff	1	Field-employee turnover	%	Y	Head of HR				
		2	Field compensation realignment	KMS	Y	Head of HR				
L3	Improve competency in key positions	1	Key positions vacant >30 days	Nos	Q	Head of HR				
L4	Transform IT to enable business	1	IT-enabled business processes	%	Y	Head of IT				
L5	Improve employee engagement	1	Employee engagement index	Index	Q	Head of HR				

INTERNAL PROCESS

LEARNING AND GROWTH

Telecom Strategy Map

Financial

- F1 — Deliver year-on-year profitable growth
- F2 — Selectively increase customer base
- F3 — Dominate RMS across all verticals and rationalize products
- F4 — Aggressively increase VAS revenues
- F5 — Minimize risks from customer churn, revenue leakage, and bad debts

Customer

- C1 — ABC provides me service that meet my needs
- C2 — ABC provides me an excellent experience
- C3 — I trust ABC in all my dealings
- C4 — As a premium post-paid customer, I receive priority service
- C5 — ABC is an attractive business opportunity to earn a good ROI/profit

Internal Processes

- I1 — Enhance NPD processes to develop product plans
- I2 — Develop roadmap to acquire high-value customers and increase revenue
- I3 — Enhance marketing processes
- I4 — Optimize and selectively expand channels
- I5 — Provide differentiated customer service levels and consistent processes
- I6 — Improve policies, processes, and accountability

Learning & Growth

- L1 — Develop HR mechanisms to improve customer orientation and team work
- L2 — Focus on training of all business partners
- L3 — Improve quality of MIS, and level of automation / IT
- L4 — Implement effective PMS, and career roadmap

Telecom Scorecard

Object #		Objective		Measures	Unit	Freq	Objective Owner	Month		YTD	
								Act	Tgt	Act	Tgt
FINANCIAL	F1	Deliver year-on-year-profitable growth	1	EBITDA	USD Mn	M	CEO				
			2	Revenue growth	%	M	VP-Mktg				
	F2	Selectively increase customer base	1	New subscribers market share	%	M	VP-Sales				
	F3	Dominate RMS across all verticals and rationalize products	1	Revenue market share	%	M	VP-Mktg				
	F4	Aggressively increase VAS revenues	1	VAS as a % of sales	%	M					
	F5	Minimize risks from customer churn, revenue leakage, and bad debts	1	Revenue leakage as a % of sales	%	M	CFO				
			2	Churn as a % of sales	%	M	VP-CSD				
			3	Bad debt as a % of sales	%	M					
CUSTOMER	C1	ABC provides me service that meets my needs	1	CSSM	No.	M	VP-Mktg				
	C2	ABC provides me an excellent experience	1	CSSM	No.	M	CEO				
	C3	I trust ABC in all my dealings	1	CSSM	%	Q	CFO / VP-CSD				
	C4	As a premium post-paid customer, I receive priority service	1	Differentiated SLA adherence	No.	M	VP-Sales				
	C5	ABC is an attractive business opportunity to earn a good and ROI/profit	1	Channel survey	No.	M	VP-Sales				

Object #		Objective		Measures	Unit	Freq	Objective Owner	Month		YTD	
								Act	Tgt	Act	Tgt
INTERNAL PROCESS	IP1	Enhance NPD processes to develop product plans	1	New plan revenue as a % of total revenue	USD	M	VP-Mktg				
			2	CSSM survey (new products)	No.	M					
			3	No. of plans contributing less than 5% revenue	No.	M					
	IP2	Develop roadmap to acquire high-value post-paid customers and increase revenue	1	Post-paid subs added as % of total subs added	%	M	VP-Mktg				
			2	Post-paid revenue as a % of total revenue	No.	M					
	IP3	Enhance marketing processes	1	Pre-paid profitability	USD	M	VP-Mktg				
			2	Post-paid profitability	%	M					
	IP4	Optimize and selectively expand channels	1	No. of channel partners	USD	M	VP-Sales				
			2	Compliance adherence	Index	Q					
	IP5	Provide differentiated customer service levels and consistent processes	1	TAT	No.	M	CEO				
			2	CSSM survey	No.	M					
			3	Cost per survey/transaction	USD	M					
	IP6	Improve policies, processes, and accountability	1	Churn as a % of subs base	%	M	CFO / VP-CSD				
			2	Bad debt as a % of sales	%	M					
			3	Customer complaints	No.	M					
LEARNING & GROWTH	LG1	Develop HR mechanisms to improve customer orientation and team work	1	Customer complaints	No.	M	Sr. VP-HR				
			2	Ops committee meetings	No.	M					
	LG2	Focus on training of all business partners	1	Training interactions	No.	M	Sr. VP-HR				
			2	CAR-ICE scores	No.	M					
			3	% of SLA/contractual adherence	No.	M					
	LG3	Improve quality of MIS, (especially profitability) and level of automation / IT	1	Key milestones	No.	M	VP-IT				
	LG4	Implement effective PMS, and career roadmap	1	Staff rating of PMS	No.	M	Sr. VP-HR				

Manufacturing Strategy Map

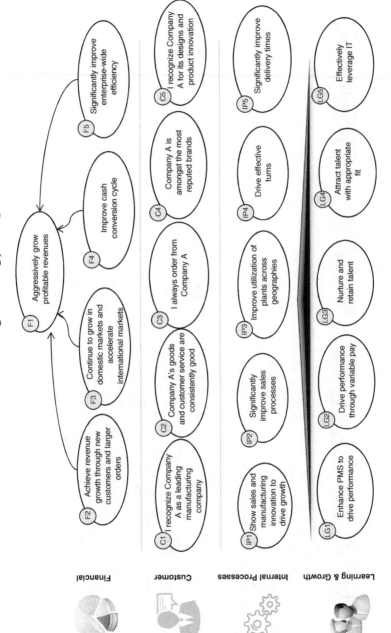

Manufacturing Scorecard

Object #		Objective		Measures	Unit	Freq	Objective Owner	Month Act	Month Tgt	YTD Act	YTD Tgt
FINANCIAL	F1	Aggressively grow profitable revenues	1	Revenue	$ Mn	M	CEO				
			2	EBITDA %	%	M	CEO				
	F2	Achieve revenue growth through customer acquisition and larger value orders	1	No. of new customers acquired	No.	M	Head of Sales				
			2	Avg. ticket size	$ Mn	Q	Head of Sales				
	F3	Continue to grow in domestic markets and accelerate sales from international markets	1	Revenue from existing markets	%	M	Head of Sales				
			2	Revenue from europe and ROW	%	M	Head of Sales				
	F4	Improve cash conversion cycle	1	Cash conversion cycle	Days	M	CFO & COO				
	F5	Significantly improve enterprise-wide efficiency	1	Total conversion cost	$ Mn	M	CFO & COO				
CUSTOMER	C1	I recognize Company A as a leading manufacturing company	1	Growth in revenue	%	M	Head of Sales				
			2	Customer survey	Index	H	Head of Sales				
	C2	Company A's goods and customer service are consistently good	1	No. of product and customer service complaints	No.	M	Head of Sales				
			2	% repeat customers	%	M	Head of Sales				
	C3	I always order from Company A	1	Incremental sales from existing customers	$ Mn	M	Head of Sales				
	C4	Company A is amongst the most reputed brands	1	Customer survey	Index	H	Head of Marketing				
			2	% Revenue from own brands	%	M	Head of Sales				
	C5	I recognize Company A for its new products	1	Revenue from new products	$ Mn	M	Head of Sales				

Object #		Objective	#	Measures	Unit	Freq	Objective Owner	Month		YTD	
								Act	Tgt	Act	Tgt
INTERNAL PROCESS	IP1	Show sales and manufacturing innovation to drive growth	1	Product innovations/ new designs	No.	M	Head of Sales & Marketing				
			2	Selling innovation	No.	M	Head of Sales				
	IP2	Significantly improve sales and marketing processes	1	Lead conversion ratio	Ratio	M	Head of Sales & Marketing				
	IP3	Improve utilization of plants across geographies and product lines	1	Capacity utilization	%	M	COO				
			2	OEE %	%	M	COO				
	IP4	Drive effective turns	1	Throughput time	Days	M	COO				
			2	Capacity utilization	%	M	COO				
	IP5	Significantly improve delivery times and adhere to quality standards	1	OTIF	%	M	COO				
			2	RFT	%	M	COO				
LEARNING & GROWTH	LG1	Enhance PMS to drive performance	1	KMS for PMS	KMS	M	Head of HR				
	LG2	Drive performance through variable pay	1	Variable to fixed comp. ratio	%	M	Head of HR				
	LG3	Attract, nurture, and retain high-performing talent	1	Attrition %	%	M	Head of HR				
			2	Employee satisfaction	Index	Q	Head of HR				
	LG4	Institutionalize PMO for new projects / initiatives	1	Number of projects under PMO	No.	Q	Head of HR				
	LG5	Effectively leverage IT	1	Nos. of IT-enabled innovations	No.	M	Head of IT				
			2	Employee usage survey score	Score	H	Head of HR				

Real Estate Strategy Map

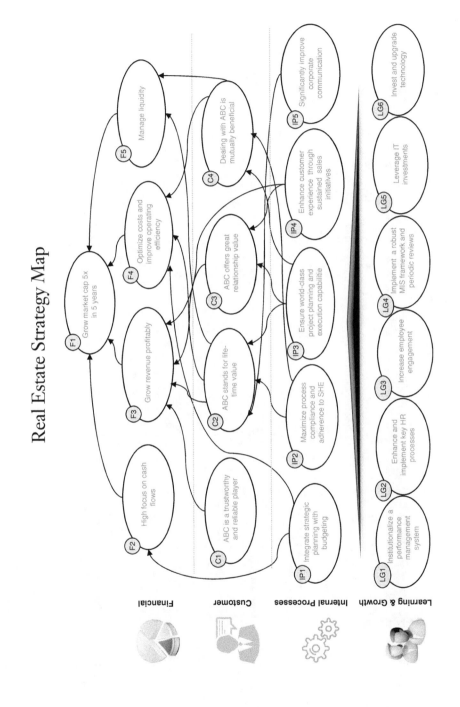

Real Estate Scorecard

Object #	Objective		Measures	Unit	Freq	Objective Owner	Month Act	Tgt	YTD Act	Tgt
FINANCIAL										
F1	Grow market cap 500% in 5 years	1	Market cap	USD	M	Chairman/MD				
		2	P/E multiple	Ratio	M	Chairman/MD				
F2	High focus on cash flows	1	Net cash flow	USD	Q	MD				
		2	Cash conversion cycle	USD	Q	Chairman/MD				
F3	Grow revenue profitably	1	EBITDA%	%	M	Chairman/MD				
		2	Growth in EBITDA	USD	M	Chairman/MD				
		3	Growth in revenue	USD	M	Chairman				
F4	Optimize costs and improve operating efficiency	1	Total expenses as % of revenue	%	M	Chairman/MD				
		2	OPEX as % of revenue	%	M	Sr. VP /AP Ops				
		3	Borrowing cost/WACC	Ratio	M	CFO				
F5	Manage liquidity	1	D/E ratio	Ratio	M	CFO				
		2	Interest coverage ratio	Ratio	M	CFO				
		3	Working capital ratio	Ratio	M	CFO				
		4	RoA	%	M	Chairman/MD				
		5	RoE	%	M	Chairman/MD				
CUSTOMER										
C1	ABC is a trustworthy and reliable real estate player	1	Customer survey	Index	HY	Chairman				
C2	ABC stands for lifetime value	1	No. of project activities on time / # total projects	%	Weekly	Sr. VP /AP Ops				
		2	% adherence to project milestones	%	M	Sr. VP /AP Ops				
		3	Quality audit	Index	M	Sr. VP /AP Ops				
		4	Project performance index	Index	M	Sr. VP /AP Ops				
C3	ABC offers great relationship value	1	Customer survey	Index	HY	Head of Sales				
		2	Complaints received	Index	Q	Head of Sales				
		3	No. of referrals received	#	Q	Head of Sales				
C4	Dealing with ABC is mutually beneficial and highly professional	1	Customer survey (contractors and vendors)	Index	HY	Sr. VP /AP Ops				
		2	No. of contracts renewed	#	Q	Sr. VP /AP Ops				

Object #	Objective		Measures	Unit	Freq	Objective Owner	Month		YTD	
							Act	Tgt	Act	Tgt
PROCESS										
P1	Integrate strategic planning with budgeting	1	KMS for budget alignment	KMS	Q	CFO				
		2	# strategy and budget review meeting conducted	#	Q	CFO				
P2	Maximize process compliance and adherence to SHE	1	Process audit comments	Index	Q	Sr. VP/AP Ops				
		2	SHE compliance audit comments	Index	Q	EMS Head				
P3	Ensure world class project management, planning, and execution capabilities	1	% variance in terms of costs	%	M	Sr. VP/AP Ops				
		2	% variance in terms of time	%	M	Sr. VP/AP Ops				
		3	Project performance index	Index	M	Sr. VP/AP Ops				
P4	Enhance customer experience through sustained sales initiatives	1	% achievement against sales target	%	M	Head of Marketing				
		2	% adherence to marketing plan	%	M	Head of Sales				
		3	% units/area sold at desired price	%	M	Head of Sales				
		4	% adherence to marketing budget	%	Q	Head of Marketing				
		5	Enquiry conversion ratio	Ratio	M	Head of Sales				
		6	Customer survey	Index	HY	Head of Sales				
P5	Significantly improve corporate communication and brand building	1	No. of corporate communication initiatives	#	Q	Head of Marketing				
		2	Customer survey	Index	HY	Head of Sales				
		3	# brand building activities undertaken	#	Q	Head of Marketing				
		4	Brand audit comments / brand equity	Index	Q	Head of Marketing				
ORGANIZATION & IT										
LG1	Design and institutionalize a performance management system	1	PMS policy compliance	%	HY	Head PMS				
		2	KMS for PMS implementation	KMS	Q	Head PMS				
		3	Employee survey	Index	HY	Head PMS				
		4	Actual variable pay out/maximum potential variable pay	%	Yearly	Head PMS				
LG2	Enhance and implement key HR processes	1	KMS on succession planning	KMS	Q	HR Head				
		2	HR process audit comments	Index	Q	HR Head				
		3	No. of HR process audit issues closed	#	Q	HR Head				
LG3	Institutionalize communication and increase employee engagement	1	# interdepartmental meetings conducted	#	HY	MD/CCO				
		2	Employee survey	Index	HY	Head HR				
		3	No. of employee engagement conducted	#	Q	Head HR				
LG4	Implement a robust MIS framework and institutionalize periodic review	1	% Compliance to MIS norms	%	M	MD/CCO				
		2	No. of scorecard meetings / department level meetings conducted & documented	#	M	CCO				
LG5	Leverage IT investment for maximum utilization through effective training	1	% adherence to IT budget	%	Q	IT Head				
		2	No. of FTEs trained on IT sys.	#	Q	Head of Training				
		3	% compliance IT training calendar	%	Q	Head of Training				
		4	User survey on IT systems and applications	#	HY	IT Head				
LG6	Invest and upgrade technology to meet contemporary standards	1	% adherence to IT budget	%	Q	IT Head				
		2	User survey on IT systems and applications	#	HY	IT Head				

Hospitality Strategy Map

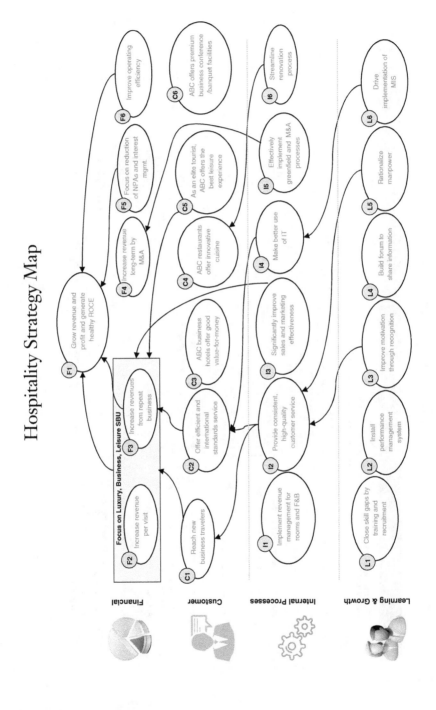

Financial

Customer

Internal Processes

Learning & Growth

Focus on Luxury, Business, Leisure SBU

F1 Grow revenue and profit and generate healthy ROCE

F2 Increase revenue per visit

F3 Increase revenues from repeat business

F4 Increase revenue long-term by M&A

F5 Focus on reduction of NPAs and interest mgmt.

F6 Improve operating efficiency

C1 Reach new business travelers

C2 Offer efficient and international standards service

C3 ABC business hotels offer good value-for-money

C4 ABC restaurants offer innovative cuisine

C5 As an elite tourist, ABC offers the best leisure experience

C6 ABC offers premium business conference /banquet facilities

I1 Implement revenue management for rooms and F&B

I2 Provide consistent, high-quality customer service

I3 Significantly improve sales and marketing effectiveness

I4 Make better use of IT

I5 Effectively implement greenfield and M&A processes

I6 Streamline renovation process

L1 Close skill gaps by training and recruitment

L2 Install performance management system

L3 Improve motivation through recognation

L4 Build forum to share information

L5 Rationalize manpower

L6 Drive implementation of MIS

199

Hospitality Scorecard

Object #		Objective		Measures	Unit	Freq	Objective Owner	Month Act	Month Tgt	YTD Act	YTD Tgt
FINANCIAL	F1	Grow revenue and profit and generate healthy ROCE	1	Total revenue growth	%	M	CEO				
			2	Total PAT growth	%	A	CEO				
			3	ROCE > WACC	%	A	CEO				
	F2	Increase revenue per visit	1	Revenue growth from luxury, business and leisure SBUs	%	M	CEO & COO				
			2	Growth in revenue per visit	%	Q	CEO & COO				
			3	Increase in guest visit duration	%	M	CEO & COO				
	F3	Increase revenues from repeat business	1	% revenues from repeat guests	%	Q	COO				
			2	% revenue growth from repeat guests	%	Q	COO				
	F4	Increase revenue long term by M&A	1	Revenues from M&A	Rs cr.	A	CEO				
			2	Number of completed M&As	No.	A	CEO				
	F5	Focus on reduction of NPAs and interest management	1	Realization from disposal of NPAs	No.	A	CFO				
			2	Interest cost % total costs	%	A	CFO				
	F6	Improve operating efficiency	1	Operating costs as% of total costs (energy, manpower, material)	%	A	COO				
			2	Variance of project cost vs. budget	Rs.cr	TBD	COO				
CUSTOMER	C1	Reach new business travelers	1	FFIT market share	%	Q	Head of Marketing				
			2	new FFIT bookings as % of new bookings	%	Q	Head of Marketing				
			3	% growth in FFIT of particular nationalities	%	Q	Head of Marketing				
	C2	Offer efficient and international standards of service	1	GSTS	Index	Q	Head of Cust. Service				
			2	Customer complaints	No.	M	Head of Cust. Service				
	C3	ABC business hotels offer good value-for-money	1	ARR competitive ratio	Ratio	M	Head of Cust. Service				
			2	GSTS	Index	Q	Head of Cust. Service				
	C4	ABC restaurants offer innovative cuisine	1	Revenue contribution from new items	%	M	Head of Cust. Service				
			2	No. of food promos/festivals	No.	Q	Head of Cust. Service				
	C5	As an elite tourist, ABC offers the best leisure experience	1	GSTS -Leisure	Index	Q	Head of Cust. Service				
	C6	ABC offers premium business conference /banquet facilities	1	Revenues from residential conferences/banquets	Rs.cr	M	COO				

Object #		Objective		Measures	Unit	Freq	Objective Owner	Month		YTD	
								Act	Tgt	Act	Tgt
PROCESS	I1	Implement revenue management for rooms and F&B	1	RevPAR for rooms	Rs	M	COO				
			2	Revenue per sq. feet	Rs	M	COO				
	I2	Provide consistent, high-quality customer service	1	GSTS	Index	Q	Head of Customer Service				
			2	No. of SLAs	No.	Q	Head of Customer Service				
			3	Adherence to SLAs	No.	Q	Head of Customer Service				
	I3	Significantly improve sales and marketing effectiveness	1	Key milestone achievement	%	-	Head of Marketing				
			2	Contribution per sales person	Rs	Q	Head of Marketing				
	I4	Make better use of IT	1	IT project delivery index	Index	Q	Head of IT				
	I5	Effectively implement greenfield and M & A processes	1	Key milestone achievement	%	TBD	CEO				
			2	Cumulative time overrun	Days	TBD	CEO				
	I6	Streamline renovation process	1	Key milestone achievement	%	TBD	COO				
			2	Cumalative time overrun	Days	TBD	COO				
ORGANIZATION & IT	L1	Close skill gaps by training and recruitment	1	No. of mandays of training (employee)	No.	M	Head of HR				
			2	Training effectiveness audit	Index	Q/A	Head of HR				
			3	No. of man-days of training (trainer)	No.	M	Head of HR				
			4	No. of position guidelines created	No.	-	Head of HR				
	L2	Install performance management system	1	Key milestone achievement	%	HY	Head of HR				
	L3	Improve motivation through recognition	1	ESI	Index	A	Head of HR				
			2	No. of rewards	No.	A	Head of HR				
			3	T/O of select personnel	%	Q	Head of HR				
	L4	Build forum to share information	1	No. of forum meetings	No.	Q	Head of HR				
	L5	Rationalize manpower	1	No. of personnel reduced	No.	HY	Head of HR				
	L6	Drive MIS implementation	1	Key milestone achievement	%	M	Head of HR				

Higher Education Strategy Map

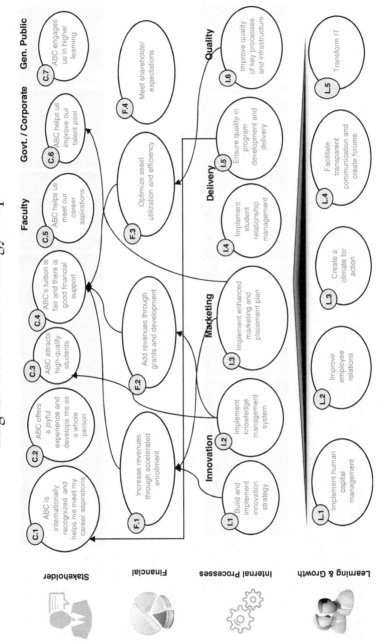

Stakeholder

	Faculty	Govt. / Corporate	Gen. Public

- **C.1** ABC is internationally recognized and helps me meet my career aspirations
- **C.2** ABC offers a joyful experience and develops me as a whole person
- **C.3** ABC attracts high-quality students
- **C.4** ABC's tuition is fair and there is good financial support
- **C.5** ABC helps us meet our career aspirations
- **C.6** ABC helps us improve our talent pool
- **C.7** ABC engages us in higher learning

Financial

- **F.1** Increase revenues through accelerated enrollment
- **F.2** Add revenues through grants and development
- **F.3** Optimize asset utilization and efficiency
- **F.4** Meet shareholder expectations

Internal Processes

- **Innovation**
  - **I.1** Build and implement innovation strategy
  - **I.2** Implement knowledge management system
- **Marketing**
  - **I.3** Implement enhanced marketing and placement plan
  - **I.4** Implement student relationship management
- **Delivery**
  - **I.5** Ensure quality in program development and delivery
- **Quality**
  - **I.6** Improve quality of key processes and infrastructure

Learning & Growth

- **L.1** Implement human capital management
- **L.2** Improve employee relations
- **L.3** Create a climate for action
- **L.4** Facilitate transparent communication and create forums
- **L.5** Transform IT

203

Higher Education Scorecard

Object #	Objective		Measures	Unit	Freq	Objective Owner	Month		YTD	
							Act	Tgt	Act	Tgt
STAKEHOLDER										
C1	ABC is internationally recognized and helps me meet my aspirations	1	Student satisfaction survey	Index	HY	Chancellor				
		2	No. of programs with international affiliations and accreditations	No.	HY	Provost				
C2	ABC offers a joyful experience and develops me as a whole person	1	No. of non-academic activities/events	No.	Q	Vice Chancellor				
C3	ABC attracts high-quality students	1	% New enrollments with > 65% HSGPA	%	Sem	Chancellor				
C4	ABC's tuition is fair and there is good financial support	1	Student satisfaction survey	Index	HY	Vice Chancellor				
		2	% enrollments with financial support	%	Sem	Chancellor				
C5	ABC helps us meet our career aspirations	1	Employee satisfaction survey	Index	HY	Chancellor				
C6	ABC helps us improve our talent pool	1	Companies visiting campus for recruitment	No.	Sem	Vice Chancellor				
		2	No. of corporate sponsored enrollments	No.	Sem	Vice Chancellor				
C7	ABC engages us in higher learning	1	Events organized/participated	No.	Q	Chancellor				
FINANCIAL ACCOUNTABILITY										
F1	Increase revenues through accelerated enrollment	1	Revenue through new enrollments	No.	Sem	Chancellor				
F2	Add revenues through grants and development	1	Revenue through grants	%	Q	Chancellor				
F3	Optimize asset utilization and efficiency	1	Cost per student	USD	M	Vice Chancellor				
F4	Meet shareholder expectations	1	Net profit	USD	M	Chancellor				

Object #		Objective		Measures	Unit	Freq	Objective Owner	Month		YTD	
								Act	Tgt	Act	Tgt
INTERNAL PROCESS	IP1	Build and implement innovation strategy	1	No. of innovations developed and launched	No.	Q	Chancellor				
	IP2	Implement knowledge management system	1	Key milestones implemented	%	Q	Provost				
	IP3	Implement enhanced marketing and placement plan	1	Total new student enrollments	No.	Sem	Chancellor				
			2	% graduating students placed	%	Sem	Vice Chancellor				
			3	Alumni events and contacts	No.	Q	Vice Chancellor				
	IP4	Implement student relationship mgmt	1	No. of student requirements addressed	No.	Q	Vice Chancellor				
	IP5	Ensure quality in program development and delivery	1	Programs/courses launched or updated	No.	HY	Provost				
			2	% Students satisfied with quality of instruction	%	Sem	Provost				
	IP6	Improve quality of key processes and infrastructure	1	No. of processes improved	No.	Q	Vice Chancellor				
ORGANIZATION & IT	L1	Implement human capital management	1	No. of employees attending training programs	No.	Q	Vice Chancellor				
			2	Papers/articles presented or published by faculty	No.	Q	Provost				
	L2	Improve employee relations	1	Employee satisfaction index	Index	HY	Chancellor				
			2	Employee turnover	%	Q	Chancellor				
	L3	Create a "climate for action"	1	% employees with IPMs	%	Q	Chancellor				
	L4	Facilitate transparent communication and create forums	1	No. of forum discussions/ meetings held	No.	M	Chancellor				
	L5	Transform IT	1	Applications new or upgraded	No.	Q	Vice Chancellor				

205

Public Sector Strategy Map

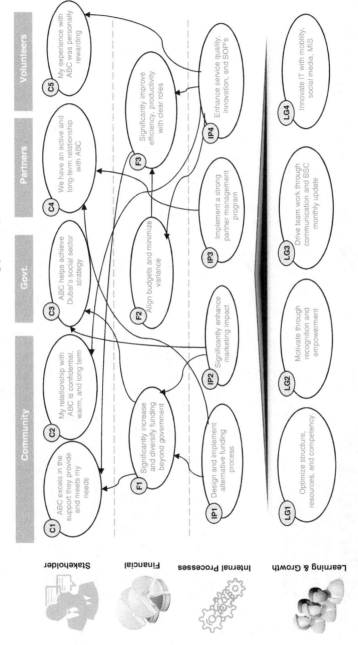

Public Sector Scorecard

Object #	Objective		Measures	Unit	Freq	Objective Owner	Month Act	Month Tgt	YTD Act	YTD Tgt
STAKEHOLDER										
C1	ABC excels in the support they provide me and meets my needs	1	Customer survey score	Index	Q	CEO Programs & Social Services				
C2	My relationship with ABC is confidential, warm, and long term	1	ABC Care Index	Index	Q	CEO Programs & Social Services				
C3	ABC helps achieve Dubai's social sector strategy (Government)	1	NGO licenses issued	%	Q	Director Licensing & Monitoring				
		2	Service provider licenses issued	%	Q					
		3	Social sectors standards	KMS	Q					
		4	% of approved polices implemented	%	Q					
C4	We have an active and long-term relationship with ABC (Partners)	1	Partner survey score	%	Y	CEO Social Planning & Development				
		2	% active to inactive partners	%	Q					
C5	My experience with ABC was personally rewarding (Volunteers)	1	Volunteer survey score	Index	Q	CEO Programs & Social Services				
		2	% active to inactive volunteers	%	Q					
FINANCIAL										
F1	Significantly increase and diversify funding beyond government	1	NGO funding	USD	Y	Director General				
		2	Funding partners	No.	Q					
F2	Align budgets and minimize variance	1	Variation to budget	%	M	CEO Corporate Services Sector				
F3	Significantly improve efficiency, productivity with clear roles	1	Cost/case	USD	M	CEO Corporate Services Sector				
		2	Cost/FTE	USD	M					
		3	Cost of service	USD	M					
		4	Cost of elderly care service	USD	M					

	Object #	Objective		Measures	Unit	Freq	Objective Owner	Month Act	Month Tgt	YTD Act	YTD Tgt
INTERNAL PROCESS	IP1	Design and implement alternative funding process	1	Fundraising meetings	No.	Q	Director General				
	IP2	Significantly enhance marketing impact	1	Free inserts	No.	Q	CEO Corporate Services Sector				
			2	Website hits	No.	M					
			3	Events	No.	Q					
			4	Social media followers	No.	M					
	IP3	Implement a strong partner mgmt. program	1	Partners' cases	No.	Q	CEO Social Planning & Development				
	IP4	Enhance service quality, innovation, and SOPs	1	SLA compliance	%	M	CEO Social Planning & Development				
			2	Cases / FTE	No.	M					
ORGANIZATION & IT	LG1	Optimize structure, resources, and competency	1	Structure optimization plan	KMS	M	CEO Corporate Services Sector				
			2	Employees with training plans	%	M					
			3	% of training program implementation	%	Q					
	LG2	Motivate through recognition and empowerment	1	Employee survey score	%	HY	CEO Corporate Services Sector				
	LG3	Drive team work through communication and BSC monthly update	1	Internal communications	%	M	CEO Corporate Services Sector				
			2	BSC Report	No.	Q	CEO Social Planning & Development				
	LG4	Innovate IT with mobility, social media, MIS	1	IT Innovation projects to be launched	KMS	M	CEO Corporate Services Sector				

209

Oil and Gas Distribution Strategy Map

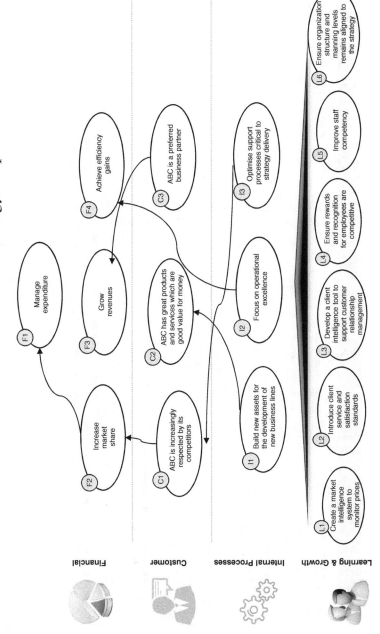

Oil and Gas Distribution Scorecard

Object #	Objective		Measures	Unit	Freq	Objective Owner	Month		YTD	
							Act	Tgt	Act	Tgt
FINANCIAL F1	Manage expenditure	1	Return on capital employed	USD Mn	M	General Manager				
		2	Progress on expenditure spend	%	M					
F2	Increase market share	1	ABC market share	%	Q	CEO & COO				
		2	% of customer feedback and their satisfaction.	%	Q					
F3	Grow revenues	1	Revenues	USD	M					
		2	New business contribution	USD	M	CEO				
		3	% of value added in existing projects	%	M					
F4	Achieve efficiency gains	1	Unit cost of all ABC activities	USD	M	COO				
CUSTOMER C1	ABC is increasingly respected by its competitors	1	ABC market share	%	Q					
		2	Net markets entered	No.	Q	CEO				
		3	New product launches	No.	Q					
C2	ABC has great products and services which are good value for money	1	Customer satisfaction statistic	Index	Q					
		2	No. of customer complaints	No.	Q	COO				
		3	Growth rate of customers	%	Q					
		4	Additional customers	No.	Q					
C3	ABC is a preferred business partner	1	Questionnaire with the partner	Index	Q	COO				
		2	No. of complaints received	No.	M					

Object #	Objective		Measures	Unit	Freq	Objective Owner	Month Act	Month Tgt	YTD Act	YTD Tgt
INTERNAL PROCESS										
IP1	Build new assets for the development of new business lines	1	No. of new assets developed	No.	Q	COO				
IP2	Focus on operational excellence	1	New improvement programs	No.	Q	CEO				
IP3	Optimize support processes critical to strategy delivery	1	Cost of service	USD	M	CEO & COO				
		2	Time to introduce a process	Days	M					
		3	BPR Success Index	Index	M					
		4	% of critical processes reengineered	%	M					
		5	% of new critical processes introduced	%	M					
		6	SLA implementation progress measure	No.	M					
		7	SLA usage measure	No.	M					
		8	Targets achieved (within 98%)	%	M					
LEARNING & GROWTH										
LG1	Create a market intelligence system to monitor prices	1	Increase the number of visits to competitors/customers	No.	Q	Head of Sales				
		2	Price monitor measure	No.	Q					
LG2	Introduce client service and satisfaction standards	1	Divisional progress index	Index	Q	Head of Sales				
LG3	Develop a client intelligence tool to support customer relationship management	1	Customer contact by sales executive	No.	M	Head of Sales				
		2	Customer complaints	No.	M					
		3	Average response time to customers	No.	M					
		4	Customer churn	No.	M					
LG4	Ensure rewards and recognition for employees are competitive	1	Yearly performance appraisal	No.	Y	Head of HR				
		2	Rewarded people	No.	Y					
LG5	Improve staff competency	1	Improve the yearly training plan	-	Y					
		2	Training courses completed	No.	Y					
		3	Development plan system for employees	%	Y					
LG6	Ensure organization structure and manning levels remain aligned to the strategy	1	Alignment index	Index	HY					
		2	OD satisfaction index	Index	HY					

Fast Food Strategy Map

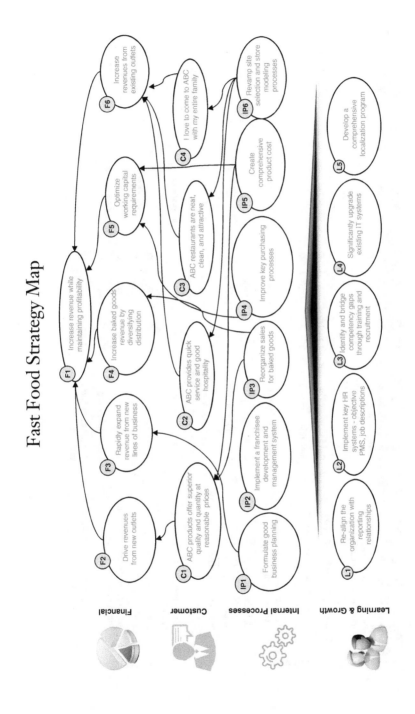

Fast Food Scorecard

Object #		Objective		Measures	Unit	Freq	Objective Owner	Month		YTD	
								Act	Tgt	Act	Tgt
FINANCIAL	F1	Increase revenue while maintaining profitability	1	Revenue growth	%	M	GM				
			2	Net profit as % of total revenues	%	M	GM				
			3	Return on capital employed	%	Q	GM				
	F2	Drive revenues from new outlets	1	Revenues from new outlet-own	$	Q	Head-Marketing				
			2	Revenues from new outlet- franchisee	$	Q	Head-Marketing				
	F3	Rapidly expand revenue from new lines of business	1	Revenue from new business	$	M	GM				
	F4	Increase baked goods revenue by diversifying distribution	1	Total baked goods revenue	$	M	Bakery GM				
	F5	Optimize working capital requirements by reducing inventory of select products	1	Current ratio	Ratio	Q	Head-Purchase				
			2	Inventory financing gap	Days	Q					
	F6	Increase revenues from existing outlets	1	Same store sales growth	%	Q	Head-Operations				
CUSTOMER	C1	ABC products offer superior quality and quantity at reasonable prices	1	Customer survey	Index	Y	Head-Marketing				
	C2	ABC provides quick service and good hospitality	1	Customer complaints	No.	Q	Head-Operations				
			2	Check-out time	Mins	Q					
	C3	ABC restaurants are neat, clean, and attractive	1	Customer walk-ins	No.	M	Head-Operations				
			2	Cleanliness index	Index	Q					
	C4	I love to come to ABC with my entire family	1	Competitive benchmarking of family sections	Index	Y	Head-Marketing				

Object #	Objective		Measures	Unit	Freq	Objective Owner	Month		YTD	
							Act	Tgt	Act	Tgt
INTERNAL PROCESS										
IP1	Formulate good business planning and product development processes	1	KMS for implementation of business planning	No.	Q	Head-Accounts/ Commissary Manager				
		2	KMS for implementation of product development	No.	Q					
IP2	Implement a franchisee development and management system	1	Profit from franchise operations	USD	M	Head-Marketing				
IP3	Reorganize sales and distribution for baked goods	1	% sales from new customers	%	M	Bakery GM				
IP4	Improve key purchasing processes and inventory management	1	Inventory days	Days	M	Head-Purchase				
		2	% of A-class vendors	%	HY					
IP5	Create comprehensive product costing processes	1	KMS for product costing system	No.	M	Head-Accounts				
IP6	Revamp site selection and store modeling processes	1	KMS for site selection and store modeling process	No.	Q	AGM				
		2	Daily revenue per cover	USD	M					
LEARNING & GROWTH										
L1	Re-align the organization with clearly defined reporting relationships	1	KMS for revised org structure	No.	Q	GM				
		2	Employee satisfaction index	Index	Y					
L2	Implement key HR systems - objective PMS, job descriptions	1	KMS for implementation of HR policies and processes	No.	Q	Head-HR				
		2	Employee turnover rate	%	Q					
L3	Identify and bridge competency gaps through training and recruitment	1	Revenue per employee	USD	HY	Head-Training				
		2	No. training days per employee	No.	Y					
L4	Significantly upgrade existing IT systems	1	KMS for implementation of systems	No.	Q	Head-Computer				
L5	Develop a comprehensive localization program	1	KMS for implementation of program	No.	Q	Head-HR				

Pharma R&D Strategy Map

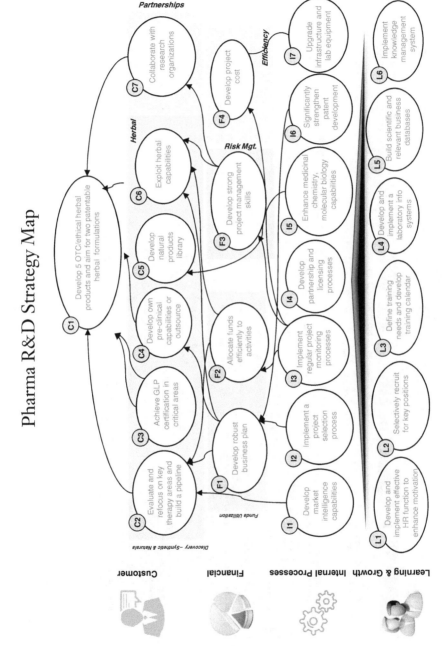

Partnerships

C7 — Collaborate with research organizations

Herbal

C6 — Exploit herbal capabilities

Efficiency

I7 — Upgrade infrastructure and lab equipment

F4 — Develop project cost

I6 — Significantly strengthen patent development

L6 — Implement knowledge management system

Risk Mgt.

F3 — Develop strong project management skills

I5 — Enhance medicinal chemistry, molecular biology capabilities

L5 — Build scientific and relevant business databases

C1 — Develop 5 OTC/ethical herbal products and aim for two patentable herbal formulations

C5 — Develop natural products library

I4 — Develop partnership and licensing processes

L4 — Develop and implement a laboratory info systems

C4 — Develop own pre-clinical capabilities or outsource

F2 — Allocate funds efficiently to activities

I3 — Implement regular project monitoring processes

L3 — Define training needs and develop training calendar

C3 — Achieve GLP certification in critical areas

I2 — Implement a project selection process

L2 — Selectively recruit for key positions

C2 — Evaluate and refocus on key therapy areas and build a pipeline

F1 — Develop robust business plan

I1 — Develop market intelligence capabilities

L1 — Develop and implement effective HR function to enhance motivation

Discovery – Synthetic & Naturals

Funds Utilization

Customer

Financial

Internal Processes

Learning & Growth

Pharma R&D Scorecard

Object #		Objective		Measures	Unit	Freq	Objective Owner	Month Act	Month Tgt	YTD Act	YTD Tgt
CUSTOMER	C1	Develop 5 OTC/ethical herbal products and aim for two patentable herbal formulations	1	No. of OTC/ethical herbal products ready	No.	Q	Head of Products				
			2	No. of patentable formulations ready	No.	Q	Head of Products				
	C2	Evaluate and refocus on key therapy areas and build a robust pipeline	1	Pipeline size in key therapy areas	USD	M	Head of Products				
			2	No. of projects with multiple targets	No.	M	Head of Products				
	C3	Implement standards and achieve GLP certification in critical areas	1	No. of key laboratories compliant with GLP	No.	Q	Head of Products				
	C4	Develop own pre-clinical capabilities or outsource	1	Key milestones	No.	Q	Head of Products				
			2	No. of outsourced partners identified	No.	Q	Head of Products				
	C5	Develop natural products library for lead discovery	1	No. of compounds in natural product library	No.	M	Head of Products				
	C6	Exploit herbal capabilities with a business plan	1	No. of herbal projects activated	No.	M	Head of Products				
	C7	Collaborate with research organizations for leads and development	1	No. of molecules in-licensed	No.	Q	Head of Products				
			2	No. of molecules licensed-out to partners	No.	Q	Head of Products				
			3	Milestone payment received	USD	Q	CFO				
FINANCIAL	F1	Develop robust business plan for increased fund levels	1	Documented business plans	No.	M	CEO				
	F2	Allocate funds efficiently to projects/ activities	1	Fund allocation variance with project plan	USD	HY	CEO & COO				
	F3	Develop strong project management skills for minimizing business risk	1	Cumulative project investment vs. milestone progress	%	M	CEO				
	F4	Develop project cost	1	Documented project cost	USD	M	COO				

Object #		Objective		Measures	Unit	Freq	Objective Owner	Month		YTD	
								Act	Tgt	Act	Tgt
INTERNAL PROCESS	I1	Develop market intelligence capabilities	1	Competitive documentation on pipeline and molecule gaps	No.	M	COO				
	I2	Implement a business-aligned project selection process	1	Defined project selection criteria	No.	Q	COO				
			2	No. of projects in focus therapy areas	No	M	COO				
	I3	Implement regular project monitoring processes for discovery	1	No. of review meetings done per project	No.	M	COO				
	I4	Develop partnership and licensing management processes	1	Key milestones/defined process document	No.	Q	COO				
	I5	Enhance medicinal chemistry, molecular biology, pharmacology capabilities and build pharmacokinetics	1	Key milestones	No.	Q	COO				
	I6	Significantly strengthen patent development	1	No. of patents filed	No.	M	Head of Products				
	I7	Upgrade infrastructure and lab equipment	1	No. of labs upgraded	No.	M	Head of Products				
			2	No. of equipment items replaced/purchased	No.	M	Head of Products				
LEARNING & GROWTH	L1	Develop and implement effective HR function to enhance motivation and retention	1	HR policy document	No.	Q	Head of HR				
			2	Employee satisfaction survey	Index	HY	Head of HR				
	L2	Selectively recruit for key positions and define job descriptions	1	No. of key positions filled	No.	M	Head of HR				
			2	No. of JDs documented	No	M	Head of HR				
	L3	Define training needs and develop training calendar	1	Training gaps identified	No.	Q	Head of HR				
			2	No. of project-related training days	No.	M	Head of HR				
	L4	Develop and implement a laboratory information systems inline with GLP	1	Key milestones	Index	Q	Head of HR				
	L5	Build scientific and relevant business information databases	1	No. of databases created/purchased	No.	HY	Head of HR				
	L6	Develop and implement knowledge management system	1	Key milestones	No.	Q	Head of HR				

IT Strategy Map

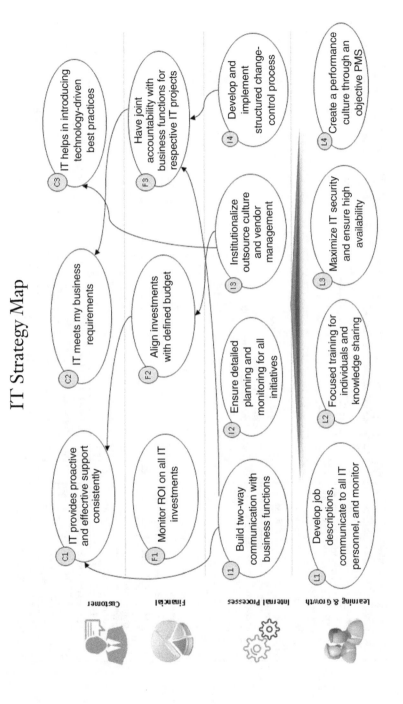

223

IT Scorecard

	Obj.#	Objective		Measure	Unit	Freq	Objective Owner	MTD Actual	MTD Target	YTD Actual	YTD Target
CUSTOMER	C1	IT provides proactive & effective support consistently	1	Avg. uptime	Mins	M	Mgr. T				
			2	No. of recurrences issues	No.	M	Mgr. IT				
	C2	IT meets my business requirements	1	Customer Satisfaction Index	Index	Q	Mgr. IT				
	C3	IT helps in introducing technology-driven best practices	1	No. of accepted technology-enabled changes	No.	M	R&D				
FINANCIAL	F1	Monitor ROI on all IT investments	1	ROI on new IT investments	%	M	Head IT				
	F2	Align investments with defined budget	1	Actual spend as % of budgeted spend	%	M	Head IT				
	F3	Have joint accountability with business functions for respective IT projects	1	Business share of financial resources/ IT share of financial resources for initiatives	%	M	Head IT				
			2	Business share of manpower resources/ IT share of manpower resources for initiatives	%	M	Head IT				
INTERNAL PROCESS	IP1	Build two-way communication with business functions	1	No. of inter departmental meetings	No.	M	Mgt. IT				
	IP2	Ensure detailed planning and monitoring	1	No. of templates defined	No.	M	Mgr. IT				
			2	% of overrun days	%	M	Mgr. IT				
	IP3	Institutionalize outsource culture and vendor management	1	% of total applications outsourced	%	M	Mgr. IT				
	IP4	Develop and implement structured-change control process	1	KMS for change control processes	KMS	M	Head IT				
L&G	L1	Develop job descriptions, communicate to all IT personnel, and monitor	1	KMS for development and communication of JDs	KMS	M	Head HR				
	L2	Focused training for individuals and knowledge sharing	1	Training Satisfaction Index	Index	Q	Head HR				
			2	Knowledge-sharing forums	No.	M	Head HR				
	L3	Maximize IT security and ensure high availability	1	% of Uptime/total time	%	M	Mgr. IT				
	L4	Create a performance culture through an objective PMS	1	% of IT staff with aligned KPIs	%	M	Head HR				

HR Strategy Map

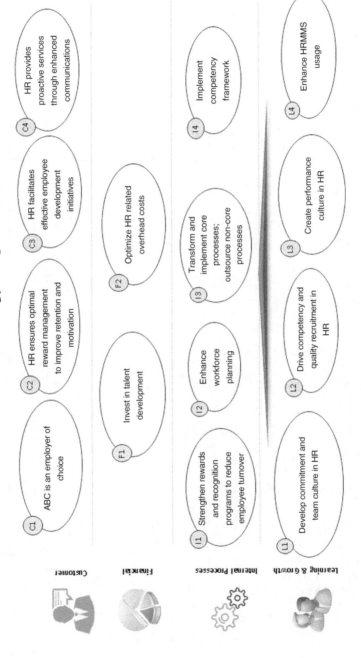

Customer

C1 — ABC is an employer of choice

C2 — HR ensures optimal reward management to improve retention and motivation

C3 — HR facilitates effective employee development initiatives

C4 — HR provides proactive services through enhanced communications

Financial

F1 — Invest in talent development

F2 — Optimize HR related overhead costs

Internal Processes

I1 — Strengthen rewards and recognition programs to reduce employee turnover

I2 — Enhance workforce planning

I3 — Transform and implement core processes; outsource non-core processes

I4 — Implement competency framework

Learning & Growth

L1 — Develop commitment and team culture in HR

L2 — Drive competency and quality recruitment in HR

L3 — Create performance culture in HR

L4 — Enhance HRMMS usage

HR Scorecard

	Obj.#	Objective	#	Measure	Unit	Freq	Objective Owner	MTD Actual	MTD Target	YTD Actual	YTD Target
CUSTOMER	C1	ABC is an employer of choice	1	Employee survey	Score	Q	HR Head				
	C2	HR ensures optimal reward management to improve retention & motivation	1	Employee survey	Score	Q	HR Head				
	C3	HR facilitates effective employee development initiatives	1	Employee Development Index	Index	Q	HR Head				
	C4	HR provides proactive services through enhanced communications	1	SLAs non-conformance	No.	M	HR Head				
			2	Communication initiatives	No.	Q	HR Head				
FINANCIAL	F1	Invest in talent development	1	Training budget for special programs	Currency	M	HR Head				
			2	Employee promotions	No.	M	HR Head				
	F2s	Optimize HR-related overhead costs	1	Reduction in HR costs	Currency	M	Head-Recruitment				
INTERNAL PROCESS	IP1	Strengthen rewards and recognition programs to reduce employee turnover	1	Attrition analysis	%	M	HR Head				
	IP2	Enhance workforce planning	1	Completed actions	KMS	M	Head-Recruitment				
	IP3	Transform and implement core processes; outsource non-core processes	1	HR process improvements completed	No.	M	HR Projects Head				
			2	No. of processes outsourced	No.	M	HR Projects Head				
	IP4	Implement competency Framework	1	Competency assessment plan	No.	M	HR Head				
L&G	L1	Develop commitment & "team culture in HR	1	HR team workshops	No.	M	HR Projects Head				
	L2	Drive competency & quality recruitment in HR	1	Training days/HR staff	%	M	Head-Recruitment				
			2	New hires	No.	Q	Head-Recruitment				
	L3	Create performance culture in HR	1	HR staff with IPMs	No.	Q	HR Head				
			2	HR initiatives completed	No.	Q	HR Head				
	L4	Enhance HRMS usage	1	HRMS usage	%	M	HR Projects Head				

226

Appendix B: Bank Case Study

Situation

ABC Bank, a leading bank with a presence in over 10 countries and a focus on corporate, commercial, and retail banking segments, wanted to have its revised strategy articulated, reflecting the new objectives that the bank was looking to achieve. This was motivated both by changes in the market environment and also the expanded reach of the bank in new emerging markets.

Significant opportunity in the marketplace was driven by a large infrastructure and real-estate boom in the home country of the bank, which supported increased penetration opportunities in the retail and wealth-management sector. The home country of the bank also had one of the highest per capita gross domestic products (GDPs), $74,000, with a population growth that was more than 15 percent per annum. The overall market conditions were also quite favorable to the banking industry, with an average return on assets (ROA) of 2.5 percent, one of the highest globally at that point in time.

However, considering that this was a few years after the 2008 global crisis, banks were generally quite skeptical about lending, since the scars of the downturn left bankers feeling risk averse. While the non-performing loan (NPL) rates in neighboring countries were operating above 7 percent, the home country of the bank was still lower than 3 percent, making it an attractive market to lend and creating a very conducive environment for growth.

Not surprisingly, the overall market was becoming fairly active, and corporate lending in the banking industry was growing at a rate of around 16 percent. However, growth in the asset book of ABC Bank was showing a declining trend, necessitating an urgent realignment of growth drivers.

Additionally, ABC Bank had the advantage of having a presence (including branch and representative office locations) in over 10 countries across three continents. Although the bank had a good international presence, both in the developed and developing markets, the share of the book in the international business remained less than 6 percent, indicating a high opportunity of penetration, particularly in the trade finance area. Most peer banks with a comparable international presence, were operating with an international asset book in the ratio of 20 to 30 percent of their overall book. Another important area of focus for ABC Bank was treasury and investments, where the growth rate of the bank was much lower, compared to its peer group. The income from financial assets or investments had significantly dropped, partly due to the share of the pie being drawn by other competitors, and partly due to the absence of product variants that could help in boosting the treasury and investments book.

The overall financial impact of these lower penetration levels was also reflected in ABC's declining income growth and a reduction in income from fees, which had dropped from its previous-year performance by over 5 percent. Meanwhile, operating expenses were much higher than at the bank's national peers, although at 35 percent this number was comparable with global benchmarks. One potential challenge was to prevent fee leakage, and the second challenge was to ensure ABC Bank's performance was aligned with the rest of the industry.

A detailed analysis of the customer book revealed that the market share of the retail book was dropping significantly. From a profitability standpoint, this was bad news because retail business was one of the bank's highest-yielding segments. The net result of all of this was a negative impact on the growth rate of the bank's overall net profits and returns, which were below the national average.

In order for ABC Bank to leverage the favorable market conditions and also ensure it could quickly capitalize on the growth trends in the country, it needed to define its strategic objectives. The best chance of moving forward was through defining a clear plan and a framework to measure performance and execution of the strategy. The Balanced Scorecard (BSC) was the most obvious tool they could use to articulate the strategic objectives of the bank, and provide a logical approach to defining performance measures. It would also help them clarify distinct objectives and set the right targets and the appropriate ownership for each of them. Since the bank had developed a scorecard about 10 years earlier, it was time for the bank to revisit this with a very specific focus, given the revised market conditions.

Solution

As part of the process in designing the BSC, a detailed review of the portfolio, the customer book, the process, the credit framework, organizational challenges, and the technology platform were studied. Some of the key challenges identified through this exercise were reviewed in detail, resulting in a formulation of the way-forward objectives that were ultimately articulated as a Strategy Map (Please refer back to Figures 8.2 and 8.3.). Some of the key areas of focus identified were:

Financial:
- The lending book was growing at a marginal 2 percent. The bank's conservative lending practices were part of the problem, so they required reevaluation.
- International investments needed to be leveraged significantly, which would also support trade finance and fee growth.
- Cost leakages required urgent attention, particularly since fee income was dropping and there was a declining trend in income growth.

Customer:

- Considering the overall market conditions, there was a significant opportunity to drive the retail share, which would also help improve overall profitability.
- The bank had combined the corporate banking segment with the small-and-medium-enterprise (SME) segment. This segment was identified as a key strategic initiative, and it was tapped for a differentiated product offering and credit approach.
- The cross-sell penetration of the bank was identified to be low, despite its potential as a key focus area. Developing this source of revenue required a focused strategic thrust.
- The bank also identified the need to improve the coverage model by better leveraging its relationship management and sales force. This would drive both share of wallet and also high-yield sales like wealth management.

Process:

- The bank had the second-largest branch network in the country, in addition to a significant international presence. The sales process was identified as needing to better align with the distribution network and branch footprint.
- Leveraging the alternative channels was key. The Internet and mobile banking platforms needed to be leveraged better. The call center was also underutilized. Driving channel penetration levels was identified as a key strategic driver, from a cost management standpoint.
- The other important focus area identified for improvement was credit. Obviously, this is central to the process framework of any bank, and ABC Bank needed to drive an effective credit-scoring approach that could differentiate for the corporate, SME, and retail segments in which the bank operated.
- Aligned to the credit process was the underwriting framework of the bank. With high volumes of paperwork and too many handoffs, the deviation rates were operating at close to

80 percent. In other words, almost 8 out of the 10 files that came up for approval required additional review on account of the deviation from pre-defined credit norms. This was identified to be another key process focus area.

Learning and Growth:
- Individual performance in alignment to the overall enterprise performance was identified as a key driver. This was not only about having the right measures to define an individual's performance, but also about ensuring that the variable compensation framework was aligned to performance.
- The bank also identified compensation as a key driver to attract and retain talent. This was important, considering that more than 40 percent of its staff had been with ABC Bank for less than one year. This was clearly an area that required strategic focus.
- More than 100 projects of various sizes and types were being executed by the bank, which meant there was an urgent need for a well-defined project management office (PMO) and effective corresponding governance.
- Just as any strategic review would result in prioritizing key initiatives, the BSC process helped to identify non-critical projects. These non-strategic efforts wasted management and delivery bandwidth that could be better used elsewhere.

Having identified the key issues that needed to be addressed, the following steps were adopted to drive an effective BSC, help articulate the bank's strategy, and also ensure all four crucial perspectives were brought into alignment:

1. Detailed one-on-one interviews were conducted with all key stakeholders of the bank, validating the observations drawn through the analysis. At the end of the day, data only gets to provide one side of the perspective—the other has to be driven by the people who own the solutions.

2. A detailed deck defining all observations was compiled and used as a prelude to drive the BSC workshop. The full-day workshop helped the team deliberate on all the key issues, and delve into each of the observation areas.

3. While it was critical to find solutions to the issues, it was more important that all 20 key members of the leadership team arrived at a consensus as to what the primary challenges were and what strategic objectives needed to be focused on.

4. Based on their discussion, the team agreed on 22 strategic objectives and articulated them on the Strategy Map. The workshop also helped identify which leaders would assume primary ownership of and responsibility for driving those objectives.

5. Each of the objectives was then mapped with corresponding metrics, both lead and lag. It was critical that the objectives and measures were developed with the stakeholders, as it not only helped define the enterprise performance measures, but also ultimately aligned with their individual performance measures as well.

6. In order for the objectives to be achieved, it was critical that each one was mapped with specific initiatives that helped in delivering those objectives. For example, to reduce the leakage in fee income, a specific initiative was identified, with a specific task force that helped focus on it.

7. The bank was then asked to define the targets for each of these measures. Some were easy, based on market performance and expected growth, while others were stretch targets to drive accelerated growth. Select objectives were also set with aspirational targets to drive overall momentum.

The bank had a very meticulous approach to measuring the overall performance, as defined by the BSC across the identified objectives. This was the basis for its monthly management reviews, ensuring focus both from a management and operational perspective.

Benefit

Through this focused exercise—and meticulous, rigorous monthly performance tracking—ABC Bank achieved a number of benefits, which were well reflected in the growth that it achieved in the subsequent years.

The asset book of the bank grew by over 80 percent in the following four years, and its international reach significantly increased to over 18 locations across 14 countries. The profitability of the bank had also improved, reflecting the bank's primary objective, to aggressively drive profitable growth.

In addition to the financial benefits that the bank achieved, the BSC exercise also helped the bank find significant benefits from an organizational perspective:

- The areas of strategic focus were agreed upon by all key stakeholders at both the management and operational levels.
- The culture of performance and measurement was instilled in employees, resulting in a significant change in the ethos and culture across the organization.
- Most importantly, individual and enterprise performance aligned, driven by well-articulated metrics mapped to defined BSC objectives. This ensured that the progress made by the organization was cohesive and synergistic.

As ABC Bank's case reveals, effective implementation of the BSC can accelerate enterprise performance and drive execution excellence.

Appendix C: Textile Company Case Study

Situation

ABC Group, is a well-diversified industrial conglomerate with interests in multiple businesses, from home textiles to paper to chemicals and energy, among others. After starting from very humble beginnings, today the ABC Group has a turnover of $1 billion. It employs over 15,000 people across four world-class, state-of-the-art manufacturing facilities. Recently, it invested $500 million in a new plant to produce a new product. This increased capacity makes ABC Group one of the largest manufacturers in the world in its segment. It has a customer base spread across more than 75 countries and six continents, and it is a key supplier to some of the leading global Fortune 500 retailers.

Over 10 years ago, the organization had restructured, from their functional structure to one based on strategic business units (SBUs). At the time, there were a number of reasons why this change made sense, including the need to treat each business as a separate entity (i.e., for separate P&L), to provide more leadership opportunities, and to increase product-line focus.

Recently the group has reorganized the management structure again, returning it to a functional structure, for the following reasons:

- Amidst this reorganization and drastic expansion, management seemed to have lost focus on the overall objectives of the group.

- Many of its performance metrics did not meet their internal target or their industry performance benchmarks. These included key financials (e.g., revenue, profitability), cash conversion cycle, order book, product quality, plant utilization, delivery schedules, inventory turns, overall productivity, creating significant enterprise risk. These needed immediate and focused attention.

- It wanted to increase focus on roles that add significant value such as: value engineering, quality, research and development (R&D), design, production planning and inventory control, strategic marketing and branding, digital marketing, sustainability, material management, centralized workshops, customer service, strategic relationships, risk, sourcing, and others.

- It wanted to increase management bandwidth and reduced dependence on particular individuals, which is where bottlenecks emerged.

- It had made significant investments in information technology (IT) in order to become a process-driven organization, more aligned with a functional structure.

- There were too many committees, forums, and management meetings. A lot of management time was spent on ad hoc and unnecessary agendas, taking their focus away from delivering what was expected of them. They needed to create a strategic, decision-making, solution-focused forum with a strategic agenda and participation.

After implementing these changes and the functional structure, the management was keen to design and implement an aligned enterprise performance management system at the corporate, department, division, and individual levels to drive strategy execution. It was also keen to institutionalize a performance-driven culture and therefore wanted to introduce performance pay (variable pay) for individuals where their key performance indicators

(KPIs) had a direct linkage to the overall organizations and their departments or divisions strategy. Additionally the group needed assistance to execute and successfully roll out these initiatives over a period of six to eight months.

Solution

The Balanced Scorecard (BSC) was identified as the solution as an enterprise performance management system to address the current challenges of the group, and also help focus on executing the strategy. A four-pronged approach was deployed to design and execute the implementation of the BSC and performance pay plans to drive enterprise performance. (Please refer back to the Manufacturing Strategy Map and Scorecard in Appendix A.)

1. **Design of corporate Strategy Map and corporate BSC to create focus at the leadership level and identify solutions for the key challenges at hand.**

   A corporate Strategy Map and a BSC enabled identification of key/prioritized objectives for the group, which were cut across financial, customer, process, learning, and growth. These were supported with extremely relevant measures. In fact, selecting the right measures was the key game changer for ABC Group. The BSC also facilitated the periodic management reporting for timely group performance reviews and supported their focus on corrective actions and strategic decision making instead of on root-cause analysis (their previous focus). The BSC served more as a strategy-deployment tool (ensuring that the strategy was being executed as envisioned) for the group and not just as another management forum or another MIS (management information system).

   The Strategy Map and Balanced Scorecard consisted of 18–20 objectives and 20–25 well-defined measures relevant to the group. Measures for each objective were carefully selected to ensure a balance between lead and lag, financial and non-financial, and quantitative and qualitative. For example, with an objective to improve cash flow, a measure on free cash flow was introduced; for the objective to profitably grow revenues, a lead indicator of sales and marketing innovations was added. To increase the average ticket size per customer, it was vital to ensure and measure customer satisfaction. Additionally, goals to improve plant and equipment utilization; overall equipment efficiency; and on-time, in-full delivery; and good quality for the first-time customer, were introduced from a manufacturing stand-point. These measures enabled the leadership to focus its attention on the key challenges and derive collective deliberation for solutions.

We assisted in finalizing and prioritizing a select set of projects and initiatives aligned to the corporate objectives (as finalized in the BSC). One of the goals of the BSC exercise was to ensure that all projects focused on achieving the group's overall strategy. We took stock of the existing internal projects, reviewed and prioritized them, and identified additional projects that were essential to successfully execute the strategy.

We used our well-tested methodology of conducting internal data analysis, selecting external market findings, and holding one-on-one meetings with key management executives to design the corporate BSC. This was then jointly finalized in a management workshop attended by key senior leaders of the group. The resulting strategy was then cascaded to the departmental level scorecards, ensuring alignment between the group's overall objectives to those of the department and eventually the employees.

2. **Design of departmental scorecards to ensure alignment between group and departmental objectives and measures.**

As the group had recently shifted to a functional-based structure, we recommended departmental scorecards rather than SBU scorecards. These departmental scorecards had specific and relevant measures embedded in them and, at the same time, were aligned to the corporate scorecard. Each scorecard outlined five to seven key strategic objectives and eight to ten measures for the department. Aligned initiatives were also prioritized.

A fast-track cascade methodology was used to design these departmental scorecards. This included a quick and strategic review of the department's performance and a preliminary meeting with the department head to understand key strategic objectives, department strengths, issues, and challenges. The implementation of these scorecards was phased in across three months, starting with marketing and manufacturing before spreading to support functions. A prioritization principal of value driver then value creator and then value enabler was used for the same.

Strategy Maps and scorecards were designed for key functional areas including marketing, manufacturing, production planning, procurement, design, strategy, finance, human resources (HR), and IT, among others. The cascading was not limited to the corporate scorecard and one level below to each department, but also to another level below to the sub-department. For example, the corporate scorecard was cascaded down to global marketing as a whole, then to country-specific marketing departments. The same approach was used for other departments. For example the corporate scorecard was cascaded down to manufacturing, then to product-specific manufacturing teams. The matrix-level cascading ensured coverage across all functions, geographies of interest, and products.

3. **Development of aligned individual performance measures (IPMs) to ensure alignment between group/ departmental and individual objectives and measures.**

Lastly the departmental and sub-departmental scorecards were cascaded down to key individuals within those departments and sub-departments. The design of these individual performance measures (IPMs) was restricted to the department and sub-department head positions only. Further cascading was done internally by the HR department.

All measures were designed within the individual's direct control and limited to four to six metrics per position. These IPMs, just like the measures for the corporate and the department had a right mix of metrics that were financial and non-financial, and leadership and operational. All measures aligned with role profiles. Appropriate weightings were identified for each measure; these were then finalized internally. A special initiative within an individual's scope of responsibility was also included in the IPMs.

We reviewed existing IPMs (whichever were available); existing job descriptions, roles, and responsibilities; and select one-on-one conversations. The IPMs were then discussed and finalized with the respective department heads.

These finalized IPMs were then embedded in the design of the variable pay plan for senior management and the design of the sales incentive scheme for the sales and marketing personnel.

4. **Design of performance pay plans (e.g., variable pay plans and sales incentives), using the IPMs and the organization's overall performance as a foundation.**

The only way to ensure success was to find a strategic measurement framework that drove enterprise performance and directly dovetailed itself into employee performance.

We therefore used a combination of organization and individual performance measures, with appropriate weightage to design the variable pay plan for the senior management group.

Additionally, a four-point rating scale was devised against the achievement percentage of each of the measure in the IPMs. Achievement target percentages were also defined. These targets were identified as aggressive but not as stretch because the aim was to establish them as achievable.

In regards to the sales incentive plan for the frontline sales staff, this was entirely based on the IPMs designed for the sales staff. Key metrics here included revenue, product mix, customer mix, and customer satisfaction.

5. **Implementation assistance across corporate BSC, department scorecards, IPMs, and variable pay plans.**

After the successful design of the corporate balanced scorecard, department scorecards, individual performance measures, and the variable pay plans, it took six months for the client to successfully roll out these initiatives.

The following activities were completed as a part of its execution.

Corporate Scorecard

1. Identified and finalized objective owners.
2. Defined and finalized formulae for all measures.
3. Created and finalized a scorecard reporting pack template.
4. Shared and finalized templates for each measure and project/ initiative.
5. Assisted in filling the scorecard.
6. Reviewed the scorecard.
7. Assisted in filling measure and project templates.
8. Facilitated the reporting of the Corporate Scorecard, along with the group's Chairman and other senior management of the organization.

Departmental Scorecard

1. Created and finalized a scorecard reporting template.
2. Defined and finalized (along with internal teams) formulae for measures across the departmental scorecards.
3. Assisted in filling (with actual data) all the departmental scorecards.
4. Reviewed all the departmental scorecards.

5. Facilitated reporting along with department heads for all the department scorecards.

Individual Performance Measures

1. Finalized weightings for each measure across IPMs. This was jointly finalized by the internal HR department.
2. Defined and finalized (along with internal teams) formulae for measures across the IPMs.
3. Assisted in filling (with actual data) all the IPMs.

Variable Pay and Sales Incentive

1. Designed implementation plan with timelines that owners and HR jointly agreed on.
2. Designed and jointly agreed-on frequently asked questions (FAQs) with answers.
3. Designed payout calculator.
4. Assisted in drafting employee communication mail.
5. Data simulated on recommended model.
6. Provided guidance to internal HR team.

Implementation included training, which was provided to key stakeholders including the HR and the strategy department teams. Well-defined and documented training manuals were also provided as a part of execution.

Benefits

It was critical to ensure the benefits from this exercise came quickly, due to mounting financial pressure that emerged from rapid organizational restructuring, leveraged plant capacity, drastic expansion, and other below-average-performing metrics across areas. The shareholder and the management teams were under severe pressure to bring the group's performance back to acceptable standards, and they had limited time to show results.

Initially there was a lot of resistance from select senior management members, as they considered this to be yet another MIS tool. But eventually management showed complete dedication and provided their sincere support in successfully rolling out these initiatives.

The results included:

1. Creation of a performance-oriented culture and a cohesive senior leadership team.
2. Alignment of goals; cascading of the corporate objectives down to departmental objectives to individual objectives.
3. Increased leadership focus on critical measures. BSC helped the organization define relevant measures addressing current challenges (e.g. cash flow, order book, product delivery, plant and equipment efficiency, right first time, rejection rate, etc.).
4. The result was a rise in EBITDA of 15 percent, a decline in finance costs by 20 percent, an increase in profit after tax by more than 100 percent, and a solid increase in cash profits.
5. Employees became more solution focused than before; the Balanced Scorecard reporting (which was held every month) forced individuals to come up with solutions rather than focusing only on root-cause analysis.
6. Enabled teams and individuals to focus on strategic priorities/projects/initiatives.
7. Created a solid platform for strategic and instant decision making; as review meetings had participation from multiple departments, management could take quick decisions on strategic areas. (I remember some policy-level decisions made during one of the review meetings when the key departments, from sales/marketing to finance to manufacturing to design to production planning, were all present in one room.)

8. Created a pay-for-performance culture where future compensation was driven primarily by performance and was variable.

9. Created multiple small, internally focused (relevant) forums to address challenges and come out with innovative solutions; rise in interdepartmental communication.

10. Through introduction of lead indicators, the management was in a better position to predict future performance.

11. Enabled the leadership team to be more proactive rather than being reactive.

12. Higher employee retention and high employee satisfaction index score.

13. On-time roll-out of critical projects (e.g. major IT implementation was rolled out on time as it was closely monitored during the monthly review meetings).

With the chairman and other senior management leading from the front and being serious about BSC execution, they found positive change. With the creation of the cascades down to the departmental and individual levels, ABC Group created a synchronized goal for the organization. Strategy has been made to work.

Appendix D: Travel and Tourism Case Study

Situation

ABC Travel and Tourism, is one of the oldest leading providers of travel and tourism (e.g., corporate, leisure travel) and related services including foreign exchange, insurance, and other services. It has been a regular recipient of multiple travel- and tourism-related awards from renowned and reputed global agencies. It operated primarily out of a brick-and-mortar model with branches and kiosks as its primary channels. It also had counters at multiple airports. It had only recently ventured into the online travel business. Its clients included leading corporations, banks, full-fledged and restricted currency exchangers, and individual travelers. ABC had expanded fast and wide, primarily through acquisitions. Recently, it had horizontally integrated by acquiring a hospitality chain and another large, leading regional travel and tour operator. It is currently identifying additional acquisition targets to become a one-stop shot for global travel and tourism.

Despite having a large presence and a large share of the market, this travel and tourism operator was facing several issues, including slow growth in revenues, primarily due to competition from low-cost online travel portals. It was struggling with increasing costs and shrinking margins, primarily through losses sustained by its brick-and-mortar outlets, along with competition from banks for low-cost foreign exchange (forex) and insurance, and several integration issues resulting from recent acquisitions. It was also facing several customer service issues.

Therefore, it was keen to conduct a detailed review of its existing business strategy, including an assessment of its operations across business lines including travel and tourism, forex, and other travel-related services, as well as a quick status check on the integration issues of its recent acquisitions. The program was aimed at developing a best-in-class enterprise performance management system using the Balanced Scorecard (BSC). This would help identify critical and strategic objectives and initiatives to be executed and implemented to significantly enhance enterprise performance.

Solution

A detailed market opportunity assessment was undertaken along with a strategic competitive environment mapping exercise. This was primarily to understand key trends and best practices in the industry. Global and regional case studies were analyzed to determine key innovations in channels and offerings, critical success factors, benchmarks, performance indicators, new avenues for growth, acquisitions and mergers, targets available in the market, regulatory changes, and other things. Based on the focused and comprehensive assessment, key implications and opportunities were outlined for the firm.

As a second step, a diagnostic strategic review was conducted of the firm's current performance from the following four perspectives: financial, customer/product, internal process/organization, and technology. This was supplemented by one-on-one meetings with select senior managers. These meetings provided a better understanding of the business, the ground realities and the challenges, not easily representable through data. The combination of strategic data review and one-on-one meetings provided deep insights of the current business. Key issues and areas of concern were outlined.

Financial:

1. Stagnating revenues; expenses growing faster than revenue. Key expenses of concern included manpower costs, promotion (new brand launch), and interest costs (primarily for funding new acquisitions and working capital requirements).

2. Shrinking margins due to rising costs; eroding profitability across business lines.

3. Rising debtor days (large corporate accounts) having an adverse impact on the firm's cash conversion cycle.

4. Some high-margin services were rendered unprofitable due to disproportionately high expenses; they needed urgent attention regarding cost reduction.

5. Significant market changes impacting business; reducing airline commissions, which were expected to go down further.

6. A quick comparative analysis also revealed that the firm was not performing well in line with key competitors; all financial metrics were below industry average.

Customer:

1. Very high customer skewing. The firm was facing high concentration risk; 3 percent of corporate customers accounted for more than 60 percent of sales. In fact, this 3 percent was made up of 10 large corporations. These were the same customers who not only accounted for large sales, but also had outstanding unpaid balances.

2. Low/declining sales per passenger; falling average ticket/transaction size. Despite increasing the product/service portfolio organically and inorganically, average sales per customer were on a decline; significant opportunities to cross-sell and upsell were not realized.

3. Declining growth in new customers. Due to poor customer service and a limited focus on call centers and online channels for sourcing, the firm was constantly losing customers, either

to its brick-and-mortar competitors or to the low-cost online travel portals.

4. Limited online sales; relatively new; needed urgent fixing. With a flurry of online travel portals, the firm's relatively mediocre portal needed a significant boost in user experience, design, and functionality.

Internal Process:

1. Low crosselling; the firm had a vision to become a one-stop shop for all the travel needs of a customer. Despite that, the average number of services sought by customers were meager. Online portals were also successful in selling bundles to customers; in fact some were successful in bundling hotel stays along with the ticketing (plus travel-related insurance).

2. The call center and web were underutilized as sales channels; they needed to be effectively leveraged as they accounted for less than 1 percent of sales.

3. There was the potential for a call center to act as a service channel.

4. A successful feet-on-street channel was missing, to be developed first for travel financial services then leveraged across other travel products.

5. Several loss-making branches.

Organization & IT:

1. Senior positions were vacant for long periods of time.

2. Low employee productivity.

3. Technology platform to be aligned for acquisitions.

4. Non-strategic management information system (MIS); needed to be cleaned and enhanced; most MIS reports not system generated.

5. Need to strengthen alternate channels; lack of business volumes from alternate channels like the Internet, IVR, and so

on. Need to enhance current internet infrastructure and migrate customer footfall from branches to Internet and IVR.

6. Potential for manpower rationalization with acquisitions.
7. Pay-for-performance culture being introduced; currently high dissatisfaction with lack of variable pay incentives.

In addition to the issues identified, a SWOT (strengths, weaknesses, opportunities, and threats) analysis was conducted for the firm.

Strengths:

1. Strong brand name.
2. High market share.
3. Value-for-money proposition for high-end travelers.
4. Gamut of services for international/corporate travelers.
5. Wide locational coverage, especially with new acquisitions.

Weaknesses:

1. High-cost culture, eroding margins in core business.
2. Low product innovation.
3. Lack of standard look and feel of processes across branches to reinforce image.
4. Back-end processes need to be streamlined for travel.
5. Corp travel: low-value accounts and high receivables.
6. Alternate channels, such as portal and DSA network, were weak.
7. Weak IT systems.
8. Speed of decision making to launch.
9. Not-so-strong relationships with hotels and airlines.

Opportunities:

1. Growing in international leisure travel.
2. Growing in domestic tourism.

3. IT portal to capture greater share of airline bookings.

4. Growing hotel, car rental services.

5. Cross sell; forex, corporate travel, and financial services hooks for cross-selling.

6. Attachment strategy: Low-margin airline booking bundled with high-margin businesses.

7. Travel-related financial services.

8. Need for a one-stop shop for all travel and travel-related services.

Threats:

1. Highly competitive and fragmented markets.

2. Ability to recognize and adapt to changing business environment; more tech-savvy portals, web offerings.

3. Leisure—highly seasonal business due to reliance on select geographies.

4. Changing regulations.

The market opportunity assessment, along with the identified issues and the firms SWOT, together enabled to outline 15–18 strategic objectives for the firm. These objectives were laid out in a Strategy Map and BSC. This was further extended to outline definitive measures with formulas for operative and timely reporting. Owners were also identified for each objective. A list of annual plans and initiatives was mapped against strategic priorities and objectives in order to successfully help the firm achieve its strategic objectives as outlined in the BSC.

In spite of an effective Balanced Scorecard design, the firm faced several implementation and reporting challenges.

• Multiple data systems.

• Measures implemented inconsistently for every meeting and formulae keep changing.

- No charting or historical analysis of the measures and data; harder to derive insights.
- Inability to slice and dice data dynamically, deep insights missing.
- Difficulty in alignment and tracking of projects.
- Last-minute changes hard to capture manually (e.g, data, measures, etc.).
- Problem is multiplied many times over when handling many cascades.

As a part of the effective execution and rollout, the firm's BSC was automated using an automation tool. This included the following:

1. **Eight dashboard sets were created for each scorecard:** Strategy Map, full BSC, finance, customer, process, learning and growth, projects, and reports.
2. **Strategy map:** Management committee members could review the map, which dynamically shows which objectives are red, yellow, and green in terms of performance.
3. **Finance, customer, process, learning and growth dashboards:** These had three widgets each and one table on key performance indicators (KPIs). These widgets allowed for easy drilling down into business lines and provided deep insights on what's driving performance and what fact-based executive decisions need to be made to improve performance.
4. **Functions:** Several functions were enabled, allowing members to create PDFs, PowerPoints, and emails of the entire dashboard and/or parts of it.
5. **Strategy-driven dashboard:** The strategic projects were also included as part of the project's dashboard.
6. **Reports:** Automatically generated BSC reporting pack for rapid distribution and archiving.

Benefit

Creation of the BSC provided necessary direction and focus to the firm through a dedicated enterprise performance management system for appropriate measurement and reporting. The management was able to take strategic decisions and measure performance using carefully selected metrics relevant to the firm and its strategic priorities.

This led to a positive shift in crucial business areas:

- Focus on high-margin business (e.g. leisure, cards) helped meet shareholder expectation.
- Improved management of business risk, especially collections/receivables and fraud.
- Development of a cost-conscious culture.
- Increased automation (web usage) for service request/lead generation for fulfillment.
- Successful implementation leading to overall operational excellence and improvement in service quality.
- Seamless integration of new acquisitions.
- Monitoring performance of the call center and eventually leveraged it for sales.
- Increased cross-selling, by including it as an important measure to drive revenue growth.
- Shutting down of loss making branches by regularly monitoring their performance; open new branches in carefully selected areas.
- Unified processes across the organization, including channels (branch, kiosk, counter, and online).

The automated BSC dashboard was easy to populate and did not heavily impact existing IT systems; it also did not call for significant investments from the firm. The scorecard coordinator was trained across multiple facets of the dashboard and it also solved the problem of multiple data sources coexisting in a firm.

More importantly, the BSC automation enabled the senior management to review the firm's performance (objectives and related measurements) on the move, allowed for trending and viewing of historic data, permitted dynamic slicing and dicing of data for deeper insights, and aided in strategic decision making. Information could be emailed, and converted to PDFs and PowerPoints, enabling addition of comments, focus on key individuals as measures could be sorted by individuals, and review could focus on certain strategic projects while ignoring others.

All of the above ensured that the firm was able to drive its overall performance.

Appendix E: Illustrative Financial Measures by Industry

Domain	Measure	Unit	Industry
F	Growth in revenue from advertising from existing clients	%	Advertising
F	Growth in revenue from non-advertising services from existing clients	%	Advertising
F	Accessories sales growth	%	Automotive
F	Gross profit of auto parts sales	Currency	Automotive
F	Growth in fleet sales	%	Automotive
F	% NPA	%	Banking & Finance
F	Book size growth	%	Banking & Finance
F	BPO revenue	Currency	Banking & Finance
F	Cards issued	No.	Banking & Finance
F	Fee income to interest income	%	Banking & Finance
F	Growth in assets	%	Banking & Finance
F	Growth in liabilities	%	Banking & Finance
F	Regional CTV volumes	No.	Consumer Durables

Domain	Measure	Unit	Industry
F	Segmental CTV volume growth	%	Consumer Durables
F	Volumes growth in B&W segment	%	Consumer Durables
F	Volumes in flat CTV	No.	Consumer Durables
F	Cost per student	Currency	Education
F	Direct cost per student	Currency	Education
F	Revenue through grants	%	Education
F	Revenue through new enrollments	No.	Education
F	Share of non-tuition/ non-grant revenues	%	Education
F	% revenue growth from repeat guests	%	Hospitality
F	% revenues from repeat guests	%	Hospitality
F	Growth in F&B profits	%	Hospitality
F	Growth in revenue per square feet	%	Hospitality
F	Growth in revenue per visit	%	Hospitality
F	Growth in RevPar	%	Hospitality
F	Growth in rooms & banquets contribution	%	Hospitality
F	Conversion cost	Currency	Industrial
F	Heat consumption	Kcal	Industrial
F	Zero liquid discharge cost	Currency	Industrial

F	Zero solid discharge cost	Currency	Industrial
F	% management services revenue	%	Oil & Gas
F	% of outsourced vehicles	%	Oil & Gas
F	% outsourcing of heavy duty drivers	%	Oil & Gas
F	Achieve efficiency gains	Currency/ MT	Oil & Gas
F	Cost per barrel (YTD)	Currency/ BBL	Oil & Gas
F	Cost per liter	Currency	Paints
F	Growth in decorative product/market	%	Paints
F	% sales from low-end instruments to total sales	%	Pharma & Medical
F	Revenues from existing formulations	Currency	Pharma & Medical
F	Avg. cost per ton (non-coal cost)	Currency	Power
F	Average realization/ hour	Currency	PR
F	% investments in energy-efficient building systems	%	Real Estate
F	Borrowing cost/ WACC	Ratio	Real Estate
F	Growth in income-generating property/ sales value	%	Real Estate

Domain	Measure	Unit	Industry
F	Occupancy rate	%	Real Estate
F	Reduction in construction cost vs. budget	Currency	Real Estate
F	% of new outlets meeting financial norms	%	Retail
F	% profits from packaging	%	Retail
F	Categories meeting margin targets	No.	Retail
F	Categories meeting revenue targets	No.	Retail

About the Author

Inspired by his father's profession, Sanjiv Anand started his career as a management consultant, and has stayed with it for over 30 years.

He is the Chairman of Cedar Management Consulting International LLC. Cedar (www.cedar-consulting.com) is an award-winning global management consulting, research, and analytics firm with a network of 16 offices globally, and over 1,000 clients. The firm was originally part of Renaissance World-wide, a $1 billion consulting firm, whose leadership included Professor Robert Kaplan of Harvard Business School, co-creator of the Balanced Scorecard (BSC).

Sanjiv is considered a Balanced Scorecard thought leader, and has over 30 years of international strategy formulation and execution experience. He has been assisting global and regional clients in the area of strategy and business transformation. He has traveled the world, executing strategy in the United States, Europe, the Middle East, India, ASEAN, China, and Japan. He has executed over 300 Balanced Scorecard designs across a wide range of industry sectors. The projects include not only design and implementation of enterprise-level Balanced Score-cards and Strategic Business Unit (SBU) Scorecards, but also Individual Scorecards (IPMs).

He has completed the Advanced Management Program at Harvard Business School. He also has a BE in Electrical Engineering, and an MBA from the Stern Graduate School of Business, New York University. He had been a member of the NYU Stern Alumni Council in New York, and a Chapter Chair of the Young Presidents Organization (YPO).

His first book, *Unlocking Human Capital to Drive Performance: A CEO Handbook*, was well received. There are also numerous articles to his credit.

His interests include music, playing the guitar, trying his hand at golf, and, more recently, spending time with the new addition to his family, his loving pet Pico.

Index